SECOND CHANCES

LIFE...AFTER...DEATH

DAVE JACKSON

SECOND CHANCES

LIFE...AFTER...DEATH

ISBN: 978-1-09832-571-8

Dave Jackson
Andover, KS. 67002
dejsurvivor@gmail.com

Cover photo credit: "EW," Eric Montgomery.
Contributing Editor, Dayna Teske.

Events in this book are based on memories from the author's perspective. The author is not a medical doctor, psychologist, or pastor, nor is his advice "medical or clinical," just his opinion. Dr. Baker and Dr. Clouse do not in any way endorse the author's medical "opinions."

Introduction

What is your **PURPOSE** in life? Can you answer quickly? I could at 30 ...and even at 40, but at 53... I could not. I'm a lifelong educator, however, I lost my purpose along the way. My focus changed from "mentoring kids and making a difference in their lives," through teaching and coaching, to "making money." I made the move from teacher to Educational Administrator because I thought it would prepare me for retirement. Instead of preparing me, it was actually killing me; physically, mentally, and spiritually.

There are tons of "self-help" and "how-to" books out there. What separates mine from those books? Look at mine as a manual about "how **NOT** to do things!" I see things in life as right or wrong, not much room for gray areas with me.

My inspiration for this book happened over an 8-month period in my life. My research is simple; it **IS** my life. My story is quite amazing! In May, I felt like it was my "calling" to tell my story of survival, so I decided to write this book. Maybe it was a spiritual calling, or a divine intervention, to give my life a real purpose. I know without a doubt that writing this book is what

I was called to do. For the first time in about 12 years, I feel very **SURE** of my purpose.

Everyone has a moment in life that will never be forgotten. My moment happened at ***6:15 a.m. on Sept. 19, 2019.*** This is the day I collapsed and died on the floor of the YMCA, but miraculously lived to tell about it. I survived a massive heart attack known as the Widowmaker!

Here is what I hope to accomplish in this book:

- ***First,*** I want to give someone a wake-up call, before it leads to a life-altering event. I will give my perspective on each of the following topics:

  - Living ***with*** and ***without*** a purpose,

  - Living ***without*** Faith and God,

  - ***Finding*** Faith and God.

  - ***Finding*** your purpose.

  - Demonstrating that ***your*** life impacts others, and the adage of "six-degrees of separation" is real; things you do each day trickle down to others, without you even realizing it.

- ***Second***, I want to give someone a real-world

experience of surviving a heart attack and having open-heart surgery. I will walk you through the surgery, recovery, rehabilitation, and what to expect each step of the way. I believe I can add some comfort and value to your outlook on the road to regaining your life. Doctors do a great job of "doctoring," however, I've found that not all communicate well with the patient and/or family about what to expect *AFTER* surgery.

Psalm 57:2 says, "I *cry out to God Most High, to God who fulfills His purpose for me.*" This is key in understanding God's purpose for your life. God has numbered your days and will fulfill every purpose He has for you.

This was one of Jeff's many motivational text messages to me about two weeks after my surgery:

"He will give you guidance and help just keep focused and don't listen to the loud voices that create doubt. Remember, that's not Him...for he whispers because he's near! You are just training to live YOUR best life yet. I believe it! Let's go! If you listen, He will tell you. You just have to be willing to do it. I think something big is in store. We will get you back and you may be the story that others need to live their lives healthy and give them hope when they can't see past their current state, recovery, etc. The comeback story is going to be classic. I'm telling you; the next chapter is going to be the best. From here out, you don't hope...you know! I know you will be back stronger than ever. STRONGER could mean in different ways than just muscle."

-Jeff Stevenson

Acknowledgment

This book is dedicated to Jeff Stevenson, my "Guardian Angel," former student, and mentor in Christ. His 3rd child was born a week before my heart attack. He became my life saver. *"Grasshopper became Sensei!"* I'm so proud of the man and father Jeff has become. I'm very grateful God placed him back in my life, and I'm forever grateful for all he has done for me...and continues to do.

More motivation from Jeff:

"Think back to the number of kids, teachers, administrators, coaches, etc., you have mentored or trained/coached...that was just the beginning. YOUR story will be able to go further. Make your so-called weakness now into your strength. Each day focusing on gains. Not overdoing, but training to build not tear down. Brick by brick. Start with the foundation and build it up. That's how we do things...I have my story and how someone like me...single mom, dad died, no money, from a town that will swallow you or put you on the wrong road...I shouldn't have made it out with everything pointed against me in most instances. However, I had a great support system surrounding myself with great coaches and mentors and I've always BELIEVED BIGGER than others. That is a lot of the battle, just believing bigger and working to do things that others aren't willing to do. I loved speaking on campuses because I saw myself in so many of these kids who for better words... were lost. Always hoped that hearing my story would spark something or change their way of thinking. YOU too have a story...it's not by coincidence. God has a bigger plan."

-Jeff Stevenson

REFLECTION: It's ironic that Jeff ended up mentoring me, after the years I spent mentoring him. I think back to mentors I had and the list is fairly short. I had two main mentors in high school. Coach Metsker and Dickie Rolls. Coach was a big influence on me, as basketball was the only sport I played. I ended up coaching it for 16 years because of him. Dickie got me interested in lifting...and the rest is history. Lol. We used to have some crazy...marathon workouts, and as far as work ethic and drive go, not many could "hang." That is why Jeff Stevenson is so fun to workout with...I taught him well. Competition from sports carries over into life.

In College, Jeff Wyrick and I became friends, and he quickly became a mentor also. I have taken advice from him for the past 34-ish years. Jeff Wyrick, Dickie and I used to have some amazing workouts also. Unreal strength and determination...both die-hard Christians.

While in Coffeyville, I worked with two coaches that became mentors and lifelong friends. Coach Wall taught me about basketball and how to get the most out of players. Coach Sills taught me to stand up for myself...period...at all cost...no questions asked. IF what I was doing was right...carry on. Lots of commonalities in all these great men. Honored to call them mentors.

Chapter 1

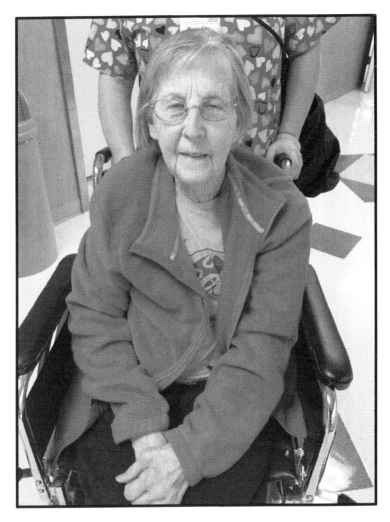

Hey Mom, I DID It!

I want to start my book by telling you about my mother, Joanne Jackson. She started my life, so it seems fitting to begin my book with her. She grew up with 7 brothers and sisters and her parents owned a grocery store, which she worked in growing up. Her mother worked in food service at a hospital, while her father ran the store. He died from a heart attack in his early 50's.

I was raised Catholic and mom always made sure I was in church each Sunday. I never read the Bible and knew very little about faith, Christianity, or even God Himself. I just knew mom wanted me to go to church so I did. Dad never attended, nor did we ever discuss it. It was just a fact of the matter.

Mom was a tough, hard working woman. She was kind and sincere to everyone she met. She was a great role model and a servant leader. She cared for everyone else first, and then **IF** there was any time or money left, she took care of herself. Funny, how neither time nor money was ever available.

Mom suffered from Dementia and Alzheimer's for many years and passed away on June 12, 2016, at the age of 79. Without a doubt, this was the saddest day in my life.

I had always told mom that I wanted to write a book someday. Now I can finally say, ***"Hey Mom, I did it!"***

REFLECTION: So many unbelievable things happened to my family and me throughout our lives. Sadly, it seemed that we did not catch many breaks. Looking back, we were pretty lucky to have each other.

Although this book is full of downers, I'll share a very happy thought. As I mentioned above, mom served others all her life. Dad was raised poor, so he wasn't a big spender, even when he made good money at Phillips. I took night classes to learn construction and eventually built my own home. My parents lived in an older home that needed a lot of work. Dad would never let me do anything to help. After he died, I built my mom a new home. If you could have seen how proud she was, it would make you smile for days. This was one of the happiest days in her life. I remember her calling friends to "take a tour" of her small house. It made me very happy to finally be able to do something for her. I had installed all new appliances for her, since cooking was her favorite hobby. She was like a kid in a candy store.

Chapter 2

Family Background

To say "stress kills" is not completely accurate. Stress, along with other things, *CAN* obviously lead to death. My life was riddled with things that would cause stress for anyone. Add in the fact that for the past 12 years I held very stressful jobs, and my diet left a lot to be desired! It was a formula for disaster.

Here is my life in a nutshell, chronologically, along with some "stressors" that changed my life drastically...numerous times along my journey. I don't want to bore anyone; however, I think at least getting a picture of how I got to this point, is very important.

I was raised by a very educated, hard-working father. My mom was also hard-working and very loving. She worked as Food Service Director at our local school for 29 years. Dad taught and coached for 10 years before he took a job with Phillips Petroleum. He had his Master's Degree and was working on his Doctorate at the University of Georgetown (through Phillips). My parents lived in Washington, D.C. for two summers, while dad worked on his Doctorate. He was a Distribution Analyst and also wrote numerous technical manuals for Phillips. He retired from Phillips and returned to his passion of teaching and coaching. He even officiated for the Big 8 Conference! He was successful at everything he did, but not necessarily *"happy."*

Dad received many awards; he was inducted into the Kansas Wrestling Hall of Fame, once as a coach, and then another time as an official. He was posthumously inducted into the National Wrestling Hall of Fame for his officiating. He retired from teaching and coaching at the age of 65. It seemed like he then quickly deteriorated from Dementia/Parkinson's Disease. He died at the age of 67, in 2001. Mom tried to take care of him. It took a toll on her...and me!

I attended a 4-year college, neither on an academic, nor athletic scholarship. I played HS basketball, but was "average" at best. When I graduated, I was really interested in weightlifting and that led to a career change. I was determined to be an architect, yet ended up with degrees in Physical Education and English. This led to a teaching/coaching career that I'm very proud of. For the first 16 years of my career, I was doing what I **loved** to do. ***It wasn't about the money; it was about helping kids.*** My first job was in Meadville, MO, where I was most likely the worst basketball coach they had seen in some time! I do believe that I was very good at helping kids and building relationships. I say that with confidence, because I'm still in contact with many of them to this day. I stayed there 3 years and worked for a great Superintendent. He supported me through some tough basketball seasons (with records something like 11-15, 12-16, and 3-20, if anyone is counting. LOL). When I left this job, I told myself, "I will never coach again." I felt like a failure at coaching.

I accepted a teaching job in Coffeyville, KS, for the next 13 years. This was a great place for me since it was 12 miles from my home town of Caney. I taught elementary Physical Education. After a year off from coaching, I was asked to coach MS basketball. I learned from two of the best coaches in the state of Kansas, Dan Wall and Frank Sills. I became a very successful coach and moved up to assistant HS coach in a couple of years. We won the 4A State Championship in boys 'basketball in 2001. It was sad that my dad wasn't alive to see it. We were good every year and I made a difference in kids' lives...***LOTS*** of kids lives.

JOURNAL PHOTO/JIM OSKISON

Field Kindley coaches Frank Sills, Dan Wall and David Jackson sit and watch silently as the 'Nado's season comes to an end.

During my time in Coffeyville, I married a local girl. We grew up together, and attended the same school in Caney. We dated, if you could call it that, in MS and then again in college. We drifted apart after college. About 6 years later, we ended up living a block apart, back in our hometown. We started hanging out with each other for all of the wrong reasons. In our small town of 1800 people, I think we ended up "settling" for each other and got married. We were divorced in 10.5 months. It was awful, mostly because we had mutual friends, which equated to half of the town. Small towns

16

like to gossip, and of course it was all my fault. I was the bad guy! It took several years for people to realize it takes two and sometimes things just don't work out. Sometimes people just aren't made for each other and that was certainly the case with us.

My sister, Karen was a year older than me. My sophomore year in college, I received a call from my dad at 4:00 a.m. on October 15, 1985. He explained that "Karen was no longer with us." She was killed in an alcohol related automobile accident. She was a passenger in the vehicle, and both lives were lost. It was a call that I will never forget. I was only 20 years old and this was really tough on my family and me.

June, 1983: This was the last "family" photo ever taken.

REFLECTION: This started the demise of my Christianity. Instead of praying to God for help, I blamed God for her death. I stopped attending church. Maybe this was a test, that I obviously failed, and maybe it was God's plan to test my strength.

MORE READING: The following Bible verses deal with "blaming God." (English Standard Version):

Proverbs 19:3	Romans 12:2
James 1:13-14	Job 13:15
1 Peter 5:8	Ephesians 6:12
1 Corinthians 10:13	John 3:36

I have two brothers. I've not seen either of them for over ten years. They were 4 and 5 years older than me. Both had athletic scholarships, one in wrestling and one in basketball. One finished college, one did not. They were in and out of trouble all through my college years. Eventually, it caught up with them and they were sentenced to federal prison for 12.5 years for manufacturing and selling methamphetamines. Mom and dad put their house up for collateral, to get my brothers out on bond. While out on bond, they were busted for meth a 2nd time. I made some calls to a friend and got the house released, but as you can imagine, it literally killed both of my parents to see this occur. I blamed my brothers for the eventual death of my father, and again blamed God for "allowing this to happen to mom and to me." Both of my brothers were still in prison when dad passed, so I was left to care for my mother. I hated them for this and never forgave them...until a few months ago.

Around 2012, mom started showing signs of Dementia/Alzheimer's and I had to be the one to make some tough decisions. I took her car away first, and eventually had to put her into an assisted living center. I was a Superintendent in a school only 18 miles away, but it was still stressful. I ended up moving in with her to "buy her some time" but I still had to go to work each day...and wonder what I would come home to. It was tough...for both of us. She accepted the life at the assisted living center and was able to extend a hand to others that were worse off ...again "servant leadership" at it's finest; ***even in the worst possible scenario, she rose to the top.***

I accepted my current job in 2014, as the Executive Director of Operations in a larger school district. The advantage of not being a Superintendent of Schools, was that I could go see mom every weekend...and I did. I would drive two hours to pick her up from the assisted living center and we would go lift weights...she LOVED lifting weights! Afterwards, we would go to lunch in Bartlesville. We did this for a couple of years, until she could no longer do so. Eventually, she collapsed on a treadmill and had to be transported to the hospital, where she stayed for about a week. ***She had a failing heart.*** It was so sad to hear. No more workouts. She pretty much gave up after that.

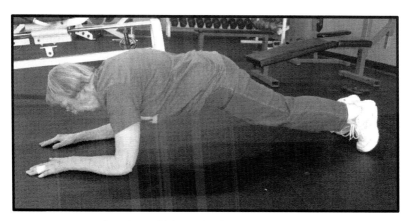

Mom showing off the "plank" at 78 years of age.

When she passed, I made it clear, through my aunt, as apparently, she had been in contact with them, that I did not want my brothers to attend her funeral. They only lived 18 miles away, but never came to see mom...not once.

REFLECTION: I later learned from one of mom's friends, that she only had *one wish*, and it was that I would make up with my brothers. So sad that it never happened while she was alive. PLEASE think about how YOUR actions impact others. *Don't let hatred impair your judgment.* Selfishness (becoming self-serving) is another great weapon of Satan. A relationship with God would have helped me fight off the devil and all of his destruction. I should have forgiven my brothers and it would have "healed" a scar for my mother and allowed her to have closure on this. Hatred and holding grudges are also HUGE stressors. I realize now, my hatred was stronger for my brothers... than my love was for my parents. *Think about that for a moment.* This was a very sad time in my life.

MORE READING: The following Bible verses deal with "hatred and holding grudges." (English Standard Version):

Ephesians 4:31-32	Matthew 18:21-35
Matthew 6:14-15	Luke 23:34
Mark 11:25	Matthew 5:23-24
Leviticus 19:18	Matthew 5:43-48
Luke 17:3-4	1 John 4:20-21
Matthew 7:1-5	Romans 14:10-12

REFLECTION: Let's talk about happiness, passion, and purpose. It seems I followed in my dad's footsteps in leaving a teaching and coaching job that I was very passionate about to enter into Educational Administration "for the money." As a building administrator, I still had lots of contact with kids and still felt like I was making a difference. I know I did in Baxter Springs, as several kids became very successful later in life, with just a nudge in the right direction and a boost in confidence. Austin, comes to mind; in middle school, I had a meeting with his parents about his behavior. After that, Austin and I spent a lot of time in the weight room. Fast-forward a couple of years and he was the top lifter in our strength program...and went on to play football at CCC & Missouri Southern, both on scholarships. He then was a grad assistant and went on to coach at Western Kentucky. This is what I was supposed to be doing... "mentoring kids."

When I moved into District Level Administration, I lost my "purpose." **No longer did I feel like I was making a difference each day.** I call this a self-made stressor. *IF* you prioritize money *OVER* happiness, you are making a huge mistake. This is another stressor that led to self-destruction.

MORE READING: The following Bible verses deal
with "the love of money." (English Standard Version):

Hebrews 13:5-6	1 Timothy 6:9-10
1 Timothy 6:17-19	Luke 12:15-21
Matthew 6:24	Matthew 6:33
Matthew 6:19-21	Proverbs 11:28
1 John 2:16	Philippians 4:19
Ecclesiastes 5:10	2 Timothy 3:2

Chapter 3

Calm Before the *Storm*

I n March (or thereabouts) of 2019, Jeff Stevenson, a former student from Coffeyville, contacted me. He and his family were living near Kansas City and he was wanting to get back to his old position in the company, to spend more time with his family. He had a timeline that he knew he could move back to the Wichita area and needed to decide (based on school districts) where to live. We visited several times and he finally made a trip out to look for housing. He purchased a house the same day. They were going to move in June/July of 2019. I was excited for them.

Jeff and I go way back. I taught him in elementary PE and worked with his mother (she was a teacher's aide) in the same building. *Jeff's father died of a heart attack (at 45) when Jeff was 4 years old.* I taught him from first through fifth grades in PE and then started coaching him in basketball when he was in 8th grade, and continued through HS. I was one of a handful of coaches that mentored Jeff. Over many years, I taught Jeff lots of things about life...giving 100% effort at everything, and believing in himself...I felt like I was a very good, positive role model for him. After HS graduation, he attended the University of Kansas. We spent many nights at basketball games together during his tenure at KU. Each summer, he came back to Coffeyville, where we would work out every weekday. We were somewhat competitive...lol...so it made for good fun. He was there when I first benched 350 pounds, and I was there when he benched 335 pounds.

REFLECTION: First of all....*IF* anyone is counting...**350** pounds is more than **335** pounds. Lol. The "mentoring" I referred to above, was my "purpose" at that time. Making a difference in Jeff's life at that time was very important to me. I knew he was going to succeed in life, without a doubt; he listened and worked very hard at everything he did. He was one of the most positive kids I ever coached. He was also a good kid and clearly had his head on straight. We never lost touch from the day he graduated high school over 15 years ago. I even read a scripture in his wedding.

Jeff graduated from KU and stayed working in the athletic office for a couple of years and eventually was hired by a commercial insurance company. He advanced in the company quickly, but the advancement meant moving his family to Minnesota. This was a long way from his mom and his wife's parents in Southeastern KS. This distance is what brought him back into my life.

Jeff and his family returned to the Wichita area in July of 2019. We started lifting in mid-July at the YMCA. It was just like old times. We both were getting really strong and putting on big-time muscle mass. We were having a blast and we were both still as competitive as ever.

After working out with Jeff for over 8 weeks, I was weighing 228 pounds, which is the biggest I'd ever been, and almost as strong as 20 years ago. Things were going well...***or so it seemed***.

Jeff took this photo on *August 16, 2019*. I weighed 220 pounds, up from 205 pounds in mid-July.

Chapter 4

A Bit More Than Partly Cloudy

Tuesday, **September 3, 2019:** Jeff and I arrived at the YMCA at our normal 5:30 a.m. time for our workout. Today's workout was focused on back and biceps. I was feeling strong, so I even brought my belt for deadlifts. We loaded up the bar to 135 pounds and warmed up. We went to 225 pounds for a couple of sets of 10. This was one lift that Jeff was always stronger than me, but I was trying to hang in there. On the 3rd set of 10 reps at 225 pounds...I felt something come over me. ***This... was... not... good.***

I told Jeff, "I'm going to head over to the mats to lay down for a minute." Jeff thought my back was hurting as it does every time we deadlifted. ***This had nothing to do with my back. I was having massive chest pains.*** I didn't say anything to anyone at first...but did finally tell Jeff, "I think I have something else going on...not sure it is my back hurting from the deadlifts." He immediately said, "I think you need to see a doctor." Of course, I completely ignored him. ***I did not need a doctor, I was fine!***

REFLECTION: *Denial* is *NOT* a form of medicine. When you have people that care about you, it is not fair to think "selfishly" and not get checked out by a doctor. Placing undue stress on others is unacceptable. *THINK* before you react. *IF* you think very hard, you will realize how you impact others. Here's a simple, yet very important question: *IF you died today, who would be impacted...and more importantly, HOW would they be impacted?*

MORE READING: The following Bible verses deal with "taking care of your body." (English Standard Version):

1 Corinthians 6:19-20	Genesis 1:27
1 Corinthians 3:16-17	Ephesians 5:29
Ephesians 2:10	1 Corinthians 15:44
1 Corinthians 12:27	1 Corinthians 9:27
1 Corinthians 6:20	Ephesians 4:16

Chapter 5

Let It Rain

Wednesday, September 4, 2019: I had talked myself into the reason for the pain from deadlifting, was due to me wearing my weightlifting belt too tight. After all, as much muscle as I had packed on over the past 8 weeks, and as strong as I was getting...there was **no way** it could be anything else. I convinced myself, without a doubt, I did not need to seek a doctor's advice.

Jeff and I arrived at the YMCA around 5:30 a.m. We started with leg curls and then moved to the leg press. I mentioned to Jeff, "I wasn't sure what was going on yesterday, but if it was anything serious, it would surely show up when we do heavy leg press." We loaded up the machine, more than we had before, and did close to 500 pounds for 10-12 reps with no problem. I felt **STRONG** and was reassured that **everything was fine.**

We decided to finish with straight legged deadlifts with dumbbells. I only grabbed 40 lb. dumbbells and started the first set. Within about 15 seconds, I got light headed and had a very bad feeling. **The SAME EXACT**

FEELING as the day before was now upon me...again. I could see the concern on Jeff's face when I went to the mats to lay down. Jeff was pretty stern with me and said, "Coach, you better go get checked out this morning!" This scared me. I agreed to get checked out.

I went home and laid down in the recliner (hoping the feeling would subside...and that I would not die right there). I texted my administrative assistant to let her know I was going to run to the doctor at 9:00 a.m. and would not be in the office for a while.

I arrived at my family practitioner's office directly at 9:00 a.m. and the receptionist told me, "We don't have any openings." I told her, "I think I'm having a heart attack, so I would like to see anyone if possible...the PA or my doctor, Kari Clouse." She immediately got up and went to the back. I sat down in the waiting room and within 30 seconds Dr. Clouse's assistant came to get me. She took me to a room, had me take my shirt off and immediately hooked up an EKG machine. I told her what happened the day before in my workout and in today's workout. I asked her, "So...what does the EKG show?" She said, ***"I don't think you really want to know. I think you are having a heart attack. Your blood pressure is 189/90."***

I was kind of numb to the thought of this actually happening. Dr. Clouse entered the room and said, ***"I think you are having a heart attack and we want to transport you to the hospital."*** I got up, put my shirt on, and told them, "There is no way I'm having a heart attack. I don't have time for this." They both just stared right through me....and Dr. Clouse eventually said, "Well, I can't force you to go. Would you at least go to Kansas Medical Center to get checked out?" I said, "Yes, I can do that but need to run by to see my boss for a minute first."

I could tell they were not pleased with me, but I was still in 100% full-on, denial mode. I was in too good of shape to be having a heart attack!!!

REFLECTION: Please see last "reflection" about denial not being a form of medicine. I don't know what else to say at this point. Fright makes people do stupid things.

I stopped by the District Office and popped into Brett's office. Brett was the Superintendent of Schools, my boss. I closed the door and said, "You are not going to believe this, but my doctor thinks I was just having a heart attack about 15 minutes ago." Brett had a look of disbelief on his face. I said, "Just to pacify her, I'm going to run out to KMC (Kansas Medical Center) and get some tests." Brett looked concerned, but I think he really thought just what I did, probably not much of a chance that it was really a heart attack.

I went to my office for a few minutes. I was really putting off going to the hospital for as long as I could. Eventually, I told June, my administrative assistant, "I may be gone for a couple of hours…and I'm not sure I'll be back today." June looked at me very oddly and asked, "What is going on?" I replied, "Nothing that I can't handle," and walked out the back door.

I arrived at the ER at KMC around 10:00 a.m. They got me right into a room and did an EKG, took blood, etc. I called Jeff to let him know what was going on. As my luck would have it, by noon, the ER doctor told me, "Everything looks fine. You know, your family doctor isn't really set up for this type of thing. To be sure everything is okay, I have scheduled you to see the cardiologist immediately. "I went to lunch as normal and then headed to the cardiologist's office at 2:00 p.m. This is the same cardiologist I saw two years prior, because my cholesterol levels were high in my health screening (at work). He had me do a stress test two years ago and I passed with flying colors...even though physically it was the hardest thing I had ever done. At the time he told me, "You have an extremely strong heart."

Today, I knew **SOMETHING** was severely wrong. Even though everything checked out at the hospital, I knew my body and knew something bad was happening...*something really bad.* The cardiologist came in and looked at everything from Dr. Clouse (she had already called him) and looked at the records from KMC and said, "You need a stress test." I told him, *"I am not doing a stress test. A stress test will kill me!"* He said it again. I told him *"NO!"* I got up and left.

REFLECTION: I'm not sure where to even begin. I made so many wrong decisions on Sept. 4th...really the only **GOOD** decision I made was **not to have the stress test.** More on that in a bit.

I kept this to myself for now. I called Jeff to let him know that everything was fine for now and that I wasn't sure what my next steps would be.

It *seems* that *my* cardiologists didn't always treat me as an individual, but as a number. They tended to be prescriptive, based on a book. If page 74 said to "give a stress test," then by all means, that is what they prescribed. In their defense, I'm sure it worked with 99.9% of their patients; I know which percentage I fall into...your mileage may vary.

REFLECTION: It is likely that if I allowed them to transport me to the hospital from Dr. Clouse's office, this would have saved me from having a future heart attack. I was still in "full-on DENIAL mode." I thought I was indestructible and didn't have time or money for these problems. As my dad would have told me, "Suck it up, and you will be fine." *I DO NOT RECOMMEND THIS TO ANYONE.*

Chapter 6

A Needed Vacation...Should I go or should I stay?

I had a vacation planned for San Diego from Sept. 12-15, 2019. I had not been to San Diego for several years and, without a doubt, it is my favorite vacation spot. A good friend, Brandon, was going with me. He had a business presentation to work on, but we still made time to hit the beach, a bay tour and some restaurants.

I met Brandon through work and we continued to build a friendship outside of work. I met his family and we hung out together, played kickball with the kids (yes, kickball...I'm pretty good, especially when his kids are 5 & 7, LOL), worked on the house a bit, and ate some brisket on occasion...heart healthy, of course. Brandon also mentored me in Christ. We started studying from a mentoring program called, "Milk for New Christians" and it is a great learning tool.

We had this vacation planned for months. I was obviously stressed and felt like this would be a well needed rest...but...I had not mentioned anything to Brandon about my week leading up to the vacation. Needless to say, off to San Diego I went anyway.

Our flight to San Diego was on a Thursday. On Friday afternoon, we had just walked a couple of miles through the Power & Light District, and I mentioned to Brandon, "If you don't mind, I need to sit down for a minute, as I am a bit winded." He didn't think much about it and we sat for a bit before moving on.

That night at supper, I **broke the news** to Brandon that, "I'm pretty sure I had a heart attack last week." I should have taken a picture of his reaction because it is hard to describe in words. LOL. Yes, I realize it is not funny, but one of mom's favorite sayings was, "You might as well laugh as cry." Think of everything she had been through and you would tend to agree.

Brandon was more concerned with what his wife would say. His wife was a former ER nurse, now a stay-at-home mom, with their 3 kids. Brandon said, *"Bethany is NOT going to be happy with you."* I felt like a 5-year old that was caught with his hand in the cookie jar. I knew I had just ruined Brandon's vacation, as he was not likely to rest very well "wondering" if I was going to die in

San Diego. We made it through the 4 days and flew back home on Sunday. Everything was fine...for the time being.

> REFLECTION: Was it good judgment to go to San Diego? I think my answer has always been similar when thinking about anything after mom died, ***"It's just me, so what does it matter?"*** Very poor answer. This is ***NOT*** how to treat friends and family. The good thing is that nobody else knew anything was going on with my health. My boss and administrative assistant thought everything checked out okay.

Chapter 7

More Poor Choices?

Jeff and I decided to take a couple of days off from lifting. We were going to start back on Wednesday. *Monday, September 16, 2019:* I received a call from the cardiologist's office asking me to schedule a stress test. I told them, "No!" I received another call from the next day, again asking me to take a stress test. I told them, "No, please do not call me about this again."

REFLECTION: This is the one area where I will defend my actions. I knew my body and **ABSOLUTELY KNEW** I would not survive a stress test. Clearly, I did not go about the process in the correct way. In hind-site, I should have gone to the ER and told them, "I had a heart attack and I'm not leaving until you do a Cath test (Cardiac Catheterization)." Would they have done it? Not likely, as most insurance companies, since they are really the ones in charge, have protocols to have a stress test done before a Cath test. It might have been worth trying.

Chapter 8

Death Becomes Me

Wednesday, September 18, 2019. I had just finished watching two episodes of *The Andy Griffith Show,* and *Gomer Pyle, U.S.M.C.* had just started. It was **8:15 p.m.** I laid back in the recliner...and suddenly...I could not move. Things seemed like they were in "slow motion." I often had nightmares like this over the past 10 years, which made me wonder, "Is this just another nightmare?" In the next few minutes, I realized it was not. I could see the TV, and I could see my phone, but I could not reach out for it....even though it was right on the arm of my recliner.

Around **8:30 p.m.,** the slow motion feeling subsided, allowing me to reach my phone. Lots of scenarios were racing through my mind; none were good. Can I get to the door? Can I get down the stairs? I live in a 3rd floor apartment, with a locked exterior stairwell door. How would anyone get to me? Can I drive? What if I call 911 and they have to break in the outside door, come up 3 flights of stairs, and then have to break in my actual apartment door? I can't afford the damages for that. *(Yes...those were really my thoughts)*. In the end, I decided to "ride it out." I laid in the chair until almost 10:00 p.m. **I had not prayed to God in a long time.** *In my mind, I believed I really had no business doing so...so I didn't,* eventually told myself, "You know, I am not ready to die, I'm not right with God, so I guess I won't ask for anything at this time." I was able to get up and walk...barely...and made it to my bed, which was about 30' away from my recliner. I laid down on the bed and stared at the ceiling fan spinning. I said to myself, *"I guess if I die tonight, I deserve to do so. I am so glad mom is not here to have to see this."* I thought I would die that night, without any doubt...I thought I would die. I was very scared.

REFLECTION: This might be the saddest part of my story. At 53 years old, I had **absolutely no** relationship with God; I mean **ZERO**! I felt like the relationship was **SO BAD**, that I did not even bother praying. *Please do not EVER think God is not listening, or that "you aren't deserving." This is simply not true.* I was so "uneducated" in Christianity, that I did not know any better.

Thursday, September 19, 2019:

I woke up the next morning at 4:50 a.m., looked at my phone, and thought, "Was this all a bad dream?" I quickly realized it was not...everything was like I had left it in the living room, even the recliner was still in the reclined position and the TV was still on. I didn't feel too bad, ***although I did feel like I cheated death...again.*** I was not thankful to God, did not say any prayers, and basically fluffed it off. Even though I was scared so badly the night before, I went on with life as if nothing ever happened.

Same day, at ***5:30 a.m.*** I headed to the YMCA. By the time I walked in, I felt a bit "off." I headed up the stairs feeling pretty lethargic, although it was very early! I figured it was fairly normal for me to feel that way. I did a couple of sets of leg curls before Jeff arrived and felt **absolutely horrible**. The scary feeling, I had the night before, was back again. Deep inside I knew something was terribly wrong! I was becoming more and more scared. I was so scared that I could not focus on anything other than the feeling that I had "100 pounds sitting on my chest."

Jeff arrived and I told him, "I don't feel great, so I think I'll watch you do leg press." He did a few sets and talked to me the entire time. I could tell he was worried about me, just by the look on his face. I found myself standing next to the leg press...hanging on to it with a one-handed death grip! I felt like I could collapse at any moment.

It finally reached a point around *6:10 a.m.*, where I told Jeff, "Hey, I think maybe I should go get checked out again, because I think there is something **REALLY** wrong." I could see the concern on Jeff's face...and I think that scared *ME* more than anything. I mentioned to him about the "feeling of having a 100-pound plate sitting on my chest." He finished his last set, picked up his bag, and we got ready to leave. I said, "Okay, now my mouth tastes like I have a roll of pennies in it." Jeff immediately said, *"Coach, that's the sign of a heart attack. Let's get out of here and get you somewhere."* We walked down the corridor towards the stairs to the lobby...and everything was blurry and I felt as if we were walking ten miles...at about six inches per second. I remember getting to the stairs and finding them blocked off. One of the trainers, Ally, was teaching a class for a group of women, and they were running up and down the stairs. One of the ladies said, "Feel free to join in!" I remember smarting off to her, in my normal, sarcastic way of dissing on cardio, and replied, *"I don't do cardio."*

At that moment, I fell straight to the floor...landing on my back, and hitting my head. I had just suffered a massive heart attack. It was now 6:15 a.m. and I was dead on the floor at the YMCA. This moment would forever change my life.

REFLECTION: If I told you I lost complete **FAITH** and **FOUND GOD** in the same week; you wouldn't likely believe it could be true...yet it happened.

MORE READING: The following Bible verses deal with "losing faith." (English Standard Version):

Luke 8:13	Hebrews 10:35-39
Hebrews 11:1-40	John 3:16-17
2 Corinthians 5:7	Mark 16:16
James 2:5	Ephesians 2:8-9
Ephesians 6:16	Mark 10:52

MORE READING: The following Bible verses deal with "If you think God is not listening." (English Standard Version):

Jeremiah 29:11	Proverbs 3:5-6
Psalm 91:1-16	Genesis 1:27
John 15:1-27	John 3:16
John 1:1-51	Psalm 126:1-6
Psalm 40:8	Joshua 1:8

Chapter 9

Waking Up After the Heart Attack

In this chapter I will discuss things from my perspective, how I remember them, and another from what I was told by Jeff and others present that day.

Thursday, Sept. 19, 2019 at 6:17 a.m.: I remember waking up with a man and three women kneeling over me. The man was Daniel Baker, an ER Trauma Doctor, at a local hospital, who happened to be on an elliptical machine working out about 20 'from where I collapsed. One woman was from the workout group that was on the stairs. The other two women were YMCA workers. I recognized them and later learned their names were Ally and Jenna. I was hooked up to an AED and I kept hearing it say, **_"It is okay to touch the body...It is okay to touch the body...It is okay to touch the body."_**

I then saw Jeff behind them. The first thing I remember him saying is, "He will tell you that he is going to refuse treatment, but that is **NOT** going to happen."

Dr. Baker asked me, "Do you know where you are?" I said, "I am at the YMCA, and I don't know you, or you (woman in the middle), but I do know her (pointing to Ally)." Dr. Baker said, "You had a heart attack and the ambulance is on the way."

I got my bearings, and of course, the first thing that went through my mind was, how embarrassing this was. I was on the floor, blocking the stairs and making a huge scene. I asked the Doctor, "Could you please move me over there out of the traffic area? This is embarrassing." He replied, "You are fine right here." So...being the good patient that I was, I attempted to get up to my elbows on my own and **BAM...the heart attack pain hit me again.** It got my attention and scared me half to death... literally. I pulled out my phone and handed it to Jeff and told him, "Call Brett (my boss), June (my asst.), and Brandon (friend)...let them know what is going on. Let Brett know I won't be at work today." Yes...I was worried about work.

All the while, Daniel was on the phone with someone giving them my vitals and instructions for when I arrived at the ER. I remember him saying, "Get him straight in for a Cath. His vitals will show that nothing happened. They are back to normal now."

> REFLECTION: Dr. Daniel Baker is a true hero. He took charge of a situation, where he could have just minded his own business and kept on exercising. I'm forever grateful to him. He later told me that I was lifeless for 45 seconds...then took a big breath...and then lifeless for another 30 seconds. He was getting ready to manually shock me...and I woke up. I would also learn that Ally and Jenna (YMCA workers) jumped into action getting the AED asap...again...I'm forever grateful. Tristen (YMCA worker) called 911 that morning...and Jeff. All 5 of these people acted as my "Guardian Angels."

The EMT's arrived and Daniel was giving them all my information. I could hear Jeff talking to people on the phone. I heard Daniel say to Jeff, "They are taking him to Wesley Medical Center." At that time the EMT's had me on a gurney and carried me down the stairs. I got my phone back from Jeff before I left. Jeff said, "Wesley...right? I'll be right behind you and see you at the hospital. Hang in there, coach." I replied, "Yes." ***Things were about to get real.*** I don't think anything had really sunk in just yet. I felt fine...again. Yes, it knocked me down pretty big time, however, I still had some fight in me, and in my mind, I truly believed I would be back home soon. I can remember sending an email to HR on my phone in the ambulance stating, "I won't be in the office today."

We arrived at the ER and they took me to an operating type room. They had me half naked in this room with nurses and doctors just walking in and out...zero privacy...and Jeff was there with me. The first thing they did was to half-shave my groin area, so they could give me a Cath test. Yep, this was a touch on the embarrassing side, but at the time I didn't really let it bother me...although once the drugs started kicking in, I do believe I embarrassed Jeff by asking, "Is there anyone in here that has **NOT** seen me naked?" I then told the doctor, "I was supposed to have a stress test this week."

They put the needle in so the dye would run in and within about 15 seconds I remember the doctor saying, "We will be cracking you open this weekend. I asked, "What time do you want me back here Saturday?" He laughed and said, *"Oh, you won't be leaving here for a while. You have about 90%, 90%,*

80%...blockage. You will need open-heart surgery, a triple bypass. You just survived the Widowmaker. We will be cracking you open on Saturday. A stress test would have likely killed you." Now my mind was racing and I became a bit more scared the more alert I became. They pumped me full of thinners and told me I would have surgery early Saturday morning. I remember giving Jeff my keys and telling him what I needed. I know he went to my apartment, stuffed a bag full of clothes along with my razor and other toiletries, and returned to be with me.

I ended up going straight to a room in the Cardiac ICU (Intensive Care Unit). My life was a complete blur at this time. One of the first things we had to do was get a Durable Power of Attorney set up so Jeff Stevenson could make any decisions on my behalf. I felt totally helpless and worthless, so I was all for this. I did not need the stress of trying to understand everything that was going on. He had taken the week off for the birth of his 3rd child; so much for being with his wife and child. Jeff **REALLY** stepped up and took care of me. He was obviously a grown-up now and I realized I was in good hands.

I remember a nurse coming in saying, "There are a couple of people in the waiting room that want to see you, but we are not allowing visitors at this time." Jeff said that Brett and Brandon were out there, so I sent him out to give them an update. Jeff had been on the phone with Dickie (another great friend) and Jerry from Tulsa. I also remember telling Jeff, "Even when they allow visitors, I don't want any if I am peeing the bed or have no control over what is going on." I had Jeff Stevenson contact Jeff H. (my best friend on the planet) and tell him what happened, but that he also did not need to visit, as there was nothing anyone could do for me at this time.

I can remember feeling lonely and scared...for the first time in my life. Yes, I had been "scared" before...and even "lonely" but **NOTHING** like this. Jeff had gone home to be with his newborn child and family. I was there by myself. I was afraid I was going to die...I mean **REALLY** afraid. I called Wyrick...one of my closest friends who is also a huge Christian. Next to Jeff Stevenson, he's the only person that I felt had a "direct line to God." I just called to let him know what happened and honestly to tell him "I was afraid of dying."

He got on the road immediately and was by my side within 2.5 hours. He prayed for me and with me. I let him know that I was not ready or worthy of dying. He walked me through the process of "where I needed to be with God." He told me, "You have nothing to worry about, God is in control." Wyrick stayed with me for a couple of hours and then prayed with me again...and left. I had lots to think about.

> REFLECTION: This was a turning point. Wyrick convinced me that I was worthy, and that everything would be okay. Of course, once he was gone, I was right back to thinking I would die, but at least he started me thinking down the right path and I will be forever grateful for that.

Later that night, I was heavily sedated, and decided I was going to talk to God for the first time in years. No, I did not hear him speak to me and didn't even know if He was even listening, but I talked and talked and talked. It was good to get everything out. I was so thankful mom had already passed and wouldn't have to worry about me. *I prayed for God to take me that night and allow me to be with my mother.*

I also had lots of time to reflect on things. Probably the number one thing I thought about was, "What a selfish life I had led." Mom was such a "giver;" she gave anything she had to anyone in need. She was a servant leader and it came so natural to her. I had always put myself first in everything (except for my time in Coffeyville) and the thought of dying that way was awful. I know I put mom first when she was alive, but I was back to being selfish after she passed.

September 20, 2019:

The next morning, I awoke and Jeff Stevenson was already in my room. He gave me an update that my surgery would be on **Saturday, Sept. 21st**. Of course, I had visitors....Jeffrey Herard....and I remember saying, "You listen really well. I'm sure this isn't your day off." He said, "I just did what you would have done." That was the end of the conversation. We just laughed for a bit.

The next visitor was Grant Smith, one of my teachers I hired in Spearville. We are great friends and I knew I could count on him for support.

Mark Burns (a Pharmacist and one of my best friends) called and "EW," Eric Montgomery (who taught me photography) called...and I convinced both of them to stay put. Both great friends and just like family.

Jerry Stultz called (Tulsa) and I told him to stay put also. We grew up a block apart from each other and are lifelong friends. I pretty much taught him everything he knows...LOL...he will appreciate that statement. Of course, he listened about as well as Jeffrey Herard did and showed up later that night. He drove 3 hours to get to talk to me for about 10 minutes and wished me good luck for surgery. Very classy. He's not an emotional person, but he was emotional that night, and so was I. I could tell he was scared "for" me. Jerry & Cassandra, his wife, had been the only real family I had for the past couple of years; I spent every weekend with them for over a year. We "worked" on projects around the house. They really kept me occupied after my mom passed away and helped me out financially. I knew I could count on them also.

June (my administrative assistant) and her husband stopped by, and so did Ricky (district worker). Matt Krehbiel stopped by and I was sleeping, but I still count it. He will surely rate this book as "RIVETING!"...I just feel it. They were very supportive throughout the entire ordeal. Eventually, when I got out of the hospital, they brought me groceries often and checked in on me all the time. Bonnie, my other administrative assistant, was also very helpful. She and June cleaned my apartment, and although quite embarrassing, it was a necessity; I could barely get around at the time.

I know more people called, and I know Jeff Stevenson called people for me. I remember Jimmy L. called; he's a former student; Travis T. called...a long-time family friend; Ted Russell (former Lead Maintenance) called...and Dickie Rolls calling. He was a close family friend, who I've known all my life...and was my neighbor growing up, and mom's neighbor when I built her a house. I could always count on him if I needed ANYTHING. He was a great role model for me my entire life and helped me greatly after mom passed away. Again...all people I knew I could count on.

Chapter 10

Pre-Surgery

Friday, *September 20, 2019*: Later that day, I spoke with my surgeon's assistant and my surgeon. The assistant went over the procedure and it sounded pretty gruesome. They would make an 8" incision in my chest and make a "sternum cut." She talked about the timeframe and said, "You will wake up in the recovery room and then we will move you to the Cardiac ICU again."

Being an avid weightlifter, I asked, "Will I ever bench press again?" She said, "I'm glad you asked. There are several different options we need to discuss about how we bind your sternum back after surgery. Option one is kind of like a spiral notebook and is wire. I don't recommend this if you plan to bench press again. We have two other options that are better for you. Option two is a process using stainless steel cables and it is wired in a butterfly fashion. The third option is a plate. I don't think that is what you want, the cables are probably the best option if you want to bench heavy again." I replied, I'll take bench press package #2."

REFLECTION: Who would have thought you had to ask for a different procedure in order to bench press again? This is one of those "ah-ha" moments that I REALLY would have been upset, 3 months down the road, if they told me, "By the way, no more bench press for you." I'm glad I asked this question *before* the surgery."

Food was wonderful throughout my stay at Wesley Medical Center. This is a HUGE deal for anyone that knows me. According to Jerry, "I'm like a picky 6-year old," to which I always respond, "I'm an adult, I can eat what I want." Breakfast was eggs and sausage, with milk and juice. I could order off the menu for lunch and supper. I always chose the cheeseburger...not a shocker to anyone that knows me. LOL.

REFLECTION: One thing I learned from one of the surgeon's assistant was the importance of having a strong "Ejection Fracture." My EF, the day of the heart attack was 68%. According to the ER doctor, "You survived because you had a strong heart." The "reference value" (norm) of a 53-year old male is 50-55%.

Chapter 11

Surgery

*S*eptember *21, 2019:* The surgeon walked in and said, "Guess who just got reinstated?..."

Just kidding. ***Life is too short not to laugh.***

Remember that, if you remember nothing else.

Chapter 12

Recovery

September 21, 2019: I remember waking up in a recovery room having difficulty breathing. It was awful. The first person I saw when I woke up was one of the Lieutenants of the Andover Police Department. Buck looked at me and said, "How are you doing?" I couldn't talk because I had tubes stuck down my throat; another awful feeling. Everything was a blur, but I was able to give him a thumbs up.

The nurse came over and "sucked up" nasty mucus from the back of my throat, as I felt like I was drowning. She used a machine much like a dental assistant uses. She did this numerous times over the next few minutes. I can remember not being able to communicate verbally, but I could draw letters in the air. Buck was watching and I kept spelling out "S-U-C-T-I-O-N." He kept getting the nurse's attention to come do it over and over...until she finally pulled out all the tubes. I had no concept of time. I still have no idea of "when" I actually woke up, how long the surgery took, or anything of that nature. I didn't feel like it was that important then, and feel the same now. Trust me, if you ever have to go through it, you will not have any "need to know this." Time meant nothing.

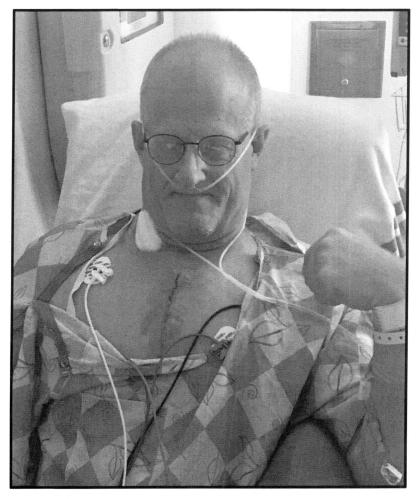

I had Buck snap a picture to send to Brett, my boss. Why was an officer from the APD there? Buck and I worked together with our SRO's (School Resource Officers) as he was the liaison between the district and the APD; we were also friends and he was checking to see that I got out of surgery okay. He is a great guy and I was impressed that he was able to make his way back to the recovery room.

> REFLECTION: I forgot this even happened until I was in a city meeting 8 months later, sitting across from Buck. We laughed about it because people never believed that Buck was actually present. They thought I was so medicated that I imagined the whole episode. It was fun to prove them wrong. Remember, "You might as well laugh as cry."

From there, I was taken to Cardiac ICU. I finally got to see Jeff Stevenson again and I was relieved. I'll be honest, he was pretty important to me in the hospital. The roles had reversed and ***Grasshopper had become Sensei!***

It wasn't like I was "up...awake...and ready to roll." I was in the most pain I'd ever experienced. To put this in perspective from what I personally had experienced as far as surgeries go (10 is the most pain, 1 is the least):

- •ACL/MCL, left knee surgery (I was around 30 years old) Pain was a 4.
- •MCL clean out (3 times over 20 years). Pain was a 2.

•Labral Tear (Rotator) left shoulder (I was around 42 years old). Pain was a 6-7 and was difficult at 42.

Open-Heart Surgery was a 10*!!!! *To be clear, when I say it was a "10," I'm referring to pain that meds just didn't touch." I sat and stared at a whiteboard on the wall in front of me for hours upon hours. Why? This board had a very important message on it. It said, "Next dose...." It was mounted right below a clock, so I could easily see how long it was until my next dose of pain medicine. The pain was brutal. I was in and out of consciousness, but when I was awake...I was in unbearable pain. If you "twitched" a muscle, your chest felt like it was going to come apart...literally; a cough felt like "death." The pain meds numbed your thoughts and "slowed" you down, but didn't do much for the pain.

REFLECTION: I suggest someone taking your phone away from you for a day or two. I found texts that my secretary called "gibberish," LOL. They looked like random letters put together with the recipients replying, "What?" Oh well...

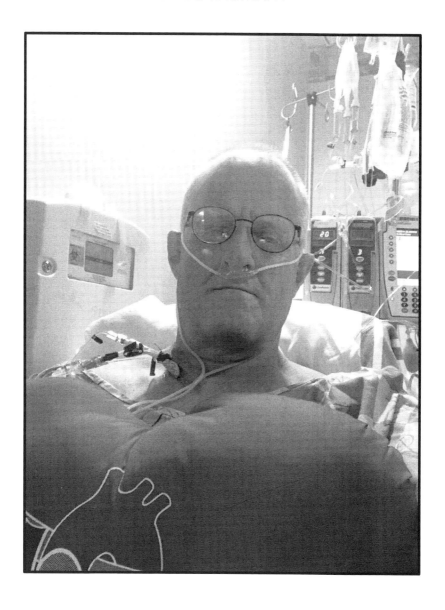

They gave me a heart-shaped, red pillow that said, "Heartfelt wishes for a speedy recovery from Wesley Medical Center Auxiliary." I thought it was a nice gesture...but didn't realize it would be a crutch for the next few weeks. They taught me to squeeze it to my chest when I coughed or sneezed. I don't mean just a little squeeze; I mean a ***"squeeze it tight OR the 8-inch incision in my chest (sternum cut) would come apart!"*** One of the most common "injuries" to open-heart surgery patients is just that...their incision comes apart and they have to be "put back together." **THIS** was not going to happen to me! Needless to say, the red pillow never left my side for the next few weeks.

I kept asking for more pain meds...they kept pointing to the board. It was an awful way to spend the day/night. I had no concept of real time after surgery. Hours ran together, and then days ran together; pretty soon I only realized it was night time because I had new nurses.

If the board said a time, you could bet your year's salary that it would be about 2 hours shy of when you **NEEDED** the meds. Even then, Percocet only killed 50% of the pain...at least it made me so nauseated that I had something else to worry about.

At least once every 15 minutes I thought, "I'm going to die...and I can't breathe." It was **AWFUL**; there is simply no other way to put it.

After surgery, my first post to Facebook was **Sunday, September 22, at 12:18 p.m.** Jeff Stevenson had been posting updates for me but I took over from there on.

The real Dave Jackson, here: I just woke up from a major nap and met with the doctor. He said all went well, but he chose to do a quadruple bypass instead of the planned triple. It must have been BOGO!!! I made it to the chair that is approximately two feet away, with the help of two nurses...and about 5 minutes. It felt like I ran a marathon. Gotta love that.

Chapter 13

Dreaming?

S till, *September 21, 2019*: When I did sleep, it was for short periods of time. One thing that kept occurring, **which I discussed with nobody** (until many weeks later) was this dream:

I could see myself lying on the floor of the YMCA with a group of people huddled around me. I looked dead. There were AED paddles hooked up to me and the doctor kept telling everyone to get back...he was getting ready to shock me. I could also see "ME" standing at the balcony of the YMCA about 50 feet east of the group and my dead body on the floor. I was visiting with a male figure that was floating a few feet away from the balcony. He was dressed in a white robe and had gray hair and a beard. I presume this was an angel or even God Himself. I could not hear what the conversation was about, but I could tell it was serious. Then...I woke up.

Over the next month, I dreamed this at least a dozen times. I was unsure of the meaning, but it would become clear very soon.

Chapter 14

Pain Management

September 22, 2019: I figured out pretty quickly that MOST of my pain was coming from two areas; my chest and my abdomen. I could understand the chest, as they just sawed my sternum in two. I couldn't understand my abdominal pains, so I asked. The nurse said the drain tubes (plural in my situation; some doctors use one, mine used two) were coiled around, inside my skin, and pressing against everything, thus, where the pain was coming from. I asked them, "When can you remove these tubes?" The nurse replied, "As soon as they are no longer draining." By the end of the night, I asked them to remove the tubes. They did so. **UNREAL** is how I would describe the "before and after" impact. The pain was gone immediately. Don't get me wrong, I still felt like I had an 8-inch cut in my sternum...**because I had an 8-inch cut in my sternum!** This was about a 50% relief.

There wasn't a drug they gave me that really killed all the pain. Percocet made me not know where I was or what I was doing...kind of a numb feeling...but still didn't touch the pain in the sternum cut **OR** the pain from the drain tubes. Toradol...Oxycodone...both killed the pain a little bit, but again, not the sternum cut or drain tubes.

In the end, Oxycodone became the drug of choice. Even when I was released, they prescribed 10mg at 10-12/day. I sat around "numb." No driving. Naps every hour. I had to take laxatives at the same time I took the Oxycodone; such a nice combination. At one time they had me taking over 12 medications. Please keep in mind, IF you don't ask the doctors or assistants, you will have no idea what most of these are for. After I was released, I called Mark (my friend that is a pharmacist) to at least understand what I was taking. Then I started researching each medicine to see what it was for.

> *REFLECTION:* The drain tubes are a BIG part of the pain. I suggest having the nurses monitor the drainage and have them removed as soon as they stop draining. It isn't like you'll jump up and run a marathon, however, it does allow you to "move freely around the cabin." Within another day, I was up and walking. IF you don't ask, they will only follow the "procedural manual" as with ANY other patient. I like to think that I was not just ANY other patient.

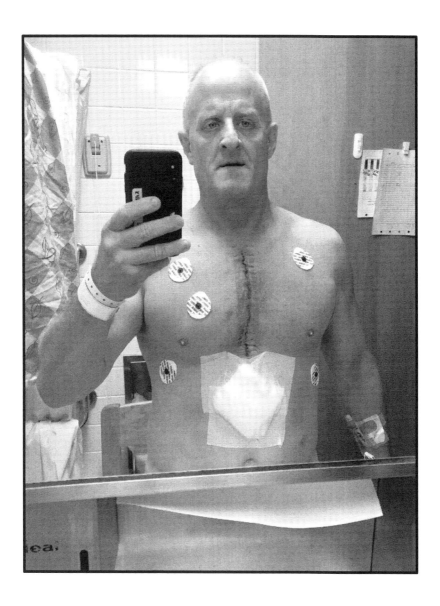

This photo was taken on **Thursday, Sept. 26, 2019**. The grimacing look shows the pain from the sternum cut. The incision/scar is **exactly** 8 inches long.

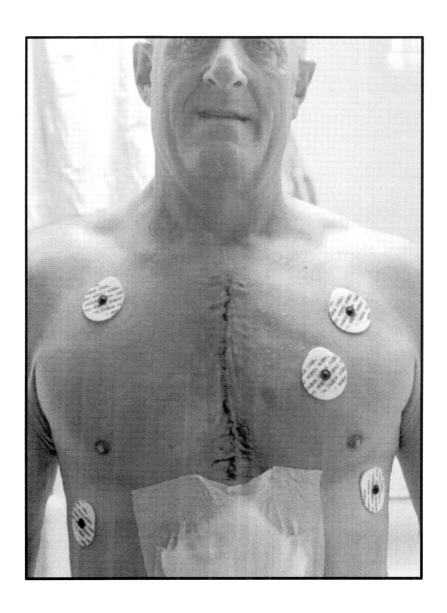

Same day, closer look.

Breathing Treatments: The doctors worry that open-heart surgery patients will get pneumonia. Although this impacts less than 5% of patients, it was still a scary thought. They gave me this little machine called an ***Incentive Spirometer***. It had a tube, a reservoir, and a small ball that raised as you breathed in, measuring your lung capacity. They told me, "We need you to do breathing treatments...at least ten times for every hour you are awake." This sounded pretty easy. I'll cut to the chase; **THIS WAS THE MOST EVIL THING I ENCOUNTERED** while in the hospital... and even at home after I was released. It was brutally painful to use.

I'm a "rule follower" so I thought I ***HAD*** to get 10 in each hour. I kept a log, made a spreadsheet, etc., because I did not want to catch pneumonia. Along with this evil machine, they encouraged me to "forcibly cough" a few times per hour. It felt like someone was cracking my chest open when I coughed or sneezed AND was jabbing a knife in my ribs at the same time. This was physically and mentally exhausting.

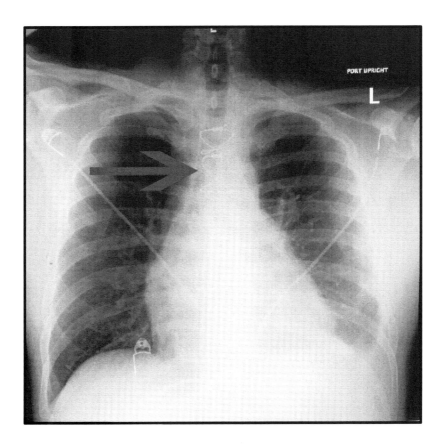

The arrow is pointing to the cables, in a butterfly fashion, that are holding my sternum cut together. One of my lungs in this photo was filled with fluid. To be honest, I never understood if it was the left or the right lung...the black part or the white part?

I followed **ALL** directions but still ended up back in the hospital with pneumonia.

REFLECTION: The fear of my lungs filling up with fluid later became a reality. Whether or not I did all the breathing treatments (IN MY OPINION...remember, I'm not a doctor) really had no bearing on one of my lungs filling up. It showed up on an X-Ray and they gave me meds for it. Eventually, it would land me back in the hospital. I read an article stating around 5% of patients end up with pneumonia. Lucky me. The breathing treatments cause your chest to expand and contract, causing all sorts of pain, and all sorts of popping and cracking sounds. It's one of those things that feels as bad as it sounds.

Chapter 15

Different Pain

September 23, 2019: The sternum cut was still painfully excruciating, but with the drain tubes out, at least it was one less thing to think about. I noticed my left groin and calf area "itched" and were painful. I didn't pay much attention when they were explaining things that were to occur during surgery. They took a pretty good size vein out of my leg to use for the bypass. Luckily, this pain did not interfere with much, it was just annoying.

There is a high percentage of people that have major issues with the leg getting infected. Many months later, it still itches, but not a big deal from my perspective. The sternum cut had some risk-factor with infection also, since it was such a large and deep cut. They had me wired, stitched, and taped...so not much was getting in or out.

I remember wearing weird looking "extremely thick" socks. They were tight...and bright yellow. They helped with circulation, as clotting was a potential issue. I kept them...because they probably cost $250!

Chapter 16

Moved Out of Cardiac ICU

September 24, 2019: I was moved out of Cardiac ICU to a normal room and could have visitors. I really didn't want a lot of visitors, and didn't want people to take that wrong. I felt like hell and needed some time to regroup before seeing people.

> REFLECTION: This is like a double-edged sword. I realized that a lot of people wanted to see me and give me encouragement, however, I was "moody" (because of the pain and the meds) and most of the time, I didn't feel like dealing with ANYONE, let alone my best friends. It is hard to explain. Please don't take it personal.

Although still a fall risk, I had to get up each day and walk. It sounded pretty easy. The effort exerted to just get out of bed was unreal. The physical therapist had to teach me to get out of bed. *I was not allowed to use my arms to pull...PERIOD*. If I did, I risked tearing open my chest...let me repeat...*I RISKED TEARING OPEN MY CHEST.*

I listened very attentively to that. I had to roll to one side, pull my knees up (good low ab workout) and use momentum to carry me up. It took some getting used to. Getting back into bed seemed to be much more of a challenge.

It was pretty discouraging to go for what they called a "walk." A physical therapist held my arm on one side the entire time. I felt like a crippled, old invalid. We would make it about 25 feet down the hall and I had to stop for two reasons: **First**, my heart rate was getting too high (from all the hard work, LOL.) and **second,** I had no lung capacity. It felt like I ran a mile and it was hard to catch my breath. Stamina was a thing of the past.

I couldn't get any of the incisions wet, so sponge baths were the norm. This was basically disgusting. I couldn't move worth a hoot, so I had complete strangers that wiped me down with some form of sterile wipes. When I say wiped me down, I mean EVERYWHERE...LOL...they had no regards for privacy, and at that point, I really didn't care...I just didn't want to be the "stinky" patient...so I let them have their way with me in the end. It also was not their first rodeo, so not a huge deal. Pain was more manageable at this time, but still hurt.

Chapter 17

Let's talk God 😊 (God Winks)

God **Wink** (Noun)

1. An event or personal experience, often identified as coincidence, so astonishing that it is seen as divine intervention, especially when perceived as an answer to a prayer.

*"So, you're telling me an ER doc, a YMCA worker who recently lost her dad from a heart deal, and the guy you work out with (had his dad die of the exact heart attack) were there for your heart attack...none of this is by coincidence." - **Jeff Stevenson***

God 😊: Jeff Stevenson, a student I taught all through elementary school, and coached through MS/HS, moved to Andover, and we started working out together...again. It had been many years ago that we worked out all the time together. I had not seen Jeff in a while, but we picked up right where we left off.

This was tough on Jeff. He watched me collapse and die on the floor of the YMCA. He has a great head on his shoulders and was there for me in the "biggest time of need in my life." Much love to Jeff!

REFLECTION: The odds of him being with me, at that particular time, are astronomical. **Remember, his father died of a heart attack when Jeff was 4.**

The following God☺'s all took place on Sept. 19, 2019, at 6:15 a.m:

God☺: While waiting at the top of the stairs of the YMCA, on our way out…the stairs were blocked by a group of people working out (running the stairs) so, Jeff and I had to wait at the top until they were done. Within 15 seconds, I was flat on my back.

REFLECTION: *Imagine what would have happened if the stairs weren't blocked and I had my heart attack ON the stairs.* I likely would have broken bones, or even my neck, along with the heart attack. Coincidence? *I think not.* Even worse, what if I had made it down the stairs and to my vehicle? What if I had made it home to my 3rd floor apartment? *I'm guessing I would not be writing this book.*

God😊: Ally (YMCA, CSCS Trainer) jumped into action immediately...running to get the AED. She was the one teaching the class to members running the stairs.

REFLECTION: I met with Ally on *Oct. 17, 2019.* I learned later, that her father passed away from cardiac complications on May 17, 2019. She shared a little bit of her story; it was awful and unexpected and she felt helpless.

When we talked about my heart attack, she said, *"When you went down...my dad's face flashed before my eyes and I knew that we had to do EVERYTHING possible to help you. Even though I couldn't be there to help my dad, I was there to help you and I'm so thankful for that. I really do think that he was watching over me that day and just put me in the right place at the right time. It's crazy how God's plan plays out sometimes. I'm thankful for that day and thankful that God put you in my life (even in the unconventional way)!"* This is one special young lady!!! Her story still sends chills up my spine. I'm so proud of her! Another hero for sure.

God☺:   Let's talk about Daniel Baker and Dr. Clouse. First of all, I've known my primary care doctor for about 4 years, but I am SOOOO impressed with her. She listens, asks questions...and gives the feeling that she "genuinely cares." I never feel like a number when visiting her office. Daniel's wife, Beth, and Kari (Dr. Clouse). ...are best friends. They all work out together and hang out all the time. Coincidence? *Again...I think not.* Dr. Clouse had Daniel text me later to set up a meeting at the YMCA.

REFLECTION: What are the odds that an ER Trauma Doctor, that deals with cardiac arrest on a weekly basis, was 20' away from me when I collapsed and died at the YMCA? *Think about that one for a minute.* Additionally, what are the odds that A, they know each other and B, they are good friends....and his wife works out with Dr. Clouse? Wow!

Chapter 18

Emotional Rollercoaster

September 25, 2019: Let's talk emotions. **BEFORE** the heart attack, if I was to rate myself from 1-10, on a scale, of "How much I showed emotion," I would have called it a low 3. This doesn't mean that I was **NOT** emotional, for goodness sake, my **FAVORITE** movies are Hallmark Movies! It just means I did not like **showing** emotions. This changed after surgery.

REFLECTION: I read a lot of articles on the "emotional energy" expended after open-heart surgery. Mood swings seemed to be the norm; depression, anxiety, loneliness, helplessness, anger, etc. I am a believer, as I experienced all of these throughout my ordeal. I did not see a correlation between the surgery date and any one of these emotions, as even months after the surgery, I still experienced all. I finally got meds for anxiety to get me started in the cardiac rehab process. *It is normal and OKAY to get help with these things.*

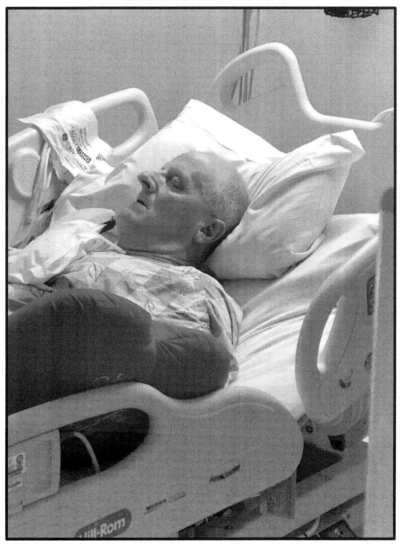

June caught a pic of me sleeping at 5:03 p.m., on **_September 25th._** I look exactly like my father, grandfather, and brother, without a doubt. Photo credit: June Brown.

Apparently, once they brought food in...I perked right up. Any food at this time sounded pretty good. I'm normally not a fan of green beans, but I was starving, so they tasted great. Photo credit: June Brown.

Chapter 19

Released from Wesley & HOME at Last!
September 26, 2019

Released from the hospital! Photo credit: June Brown.

J eff Stevenson and Wade (another former student) came to pick me up at the hospital today. This was a special day, but Wade ("Wader") and Jeff made me laugh a few times and it felt like my chest was going to crack wide open. No worries, I had my pillow!

Even though I had been taking walks in the hospital, I was not in any condition to go very far just yet. I was very independent, but now was not the time to be "that guy." The hospital did not allow me to walk out, they had to take me in a wheelchair. Once I was by the curb, I was ready to "run;" only if my body had cooperated. I felt like I had been beaten in my sleep for a few days in a row.

Once we pulled into my apartment complex, the reality that I lived on the 3rd floor hit me. Yee haw! The walk up the stairs was unbelievable. I was panting like a dog by the time I reached my apartment. I immediately headed to the recliner and sat down…then laid down…it was difficult to operate the lever of the recliner because of the pain from my sternum cut.

It took at least five minutes to catch my breath. At that time, I started to doubt whether it was a good idea that I was released from the hospital.

REFLECTION: I learned quickly that the devil wanted me to fail and give in, but it was not going to happen. I had to keep the faith and believe that I could do this...but it was pretty lonely at this time. I knew Jeff Stevenson had to be with his newborn and family (they obviously deserved him) and I would need to work some things out on my own.

Chapter 20

My First 911 Call...
Back in the Hospital...

September 29, 2019: I woke up at 12:30 a.m. and could not catch my breath. My BP wasn't high and my HR wasn't high, I simply **COULD NOT BREATHE.** The more I thought about it and tried to relax, the worse it got.

I called 911 and met the ambulance at the steps of my apartment. I texted Jeff Stevenson to let him know what was going on.

After laying in a bed for 8 hours in the ER, they finally admitted me. They ran all sorts of tests and concluded that I had pneumonia. They gave me multiple shots of what I presumed to be antibiotics.

October 1, 2019: Jeff sent me the following message when I was in the hospital, because I was having anxiety issues:

Philippians 4:6-7 (NIV)

6 Do not be anxious about anything, but in every situation, by prayer and petition, with thanksgiving present your request to God.

7 And the peace of God, which transcends all understanding, will guard your hearts and your minds in Christ Jesus.

I was released on **October 2, 2019.** Time to start over...again.

> REFLECTION: I was now a "believer" that anxiety existed. I ended up going to my primary care physician and getting some meds to get my mind off "breathing." It's not something you should have to think about.

Chapter 21

Returning to the Scene...the YMCA

Returning to the YMCA had been on my mind for quite some time. I was very hesitant to do so, but knew I had to overcome the fear...yes...fear. This is a place I visited 4 days a week for the past 6 years, but I was "fearful" of going again.

On **October 17, 2019,** I decided to go meet the people that helped save my lives. I'd seen all of them in passing, off and on, in the Y for the past few years, just a "good morning" or "good afternoon" was about it. I did not even know their names. I knew the Director through dealing with activities in our schools, so I started with a visit to his office. A woman there directed me to my three Guardian Angels (Ally, Jenna, and Tristen). I was lucky enough that all three were there the day I visited. I met each one, gave them a hug (pre-Covid 19), and had my picture taken with them. It felt like a great achievement and my fear was gone. These young people were all smiles!

Meet Ally, CSCS, USAW, Pn1 Fitness Director at the YMCA.

Meet Jenna, a Trainer at the YMCA.

Meet Tristen, a former YMCA worker.

While at the YMCA, I took many pictures of the exact spot I collapsed (large red arrow above) from all directions. When I got home, my project for the day was to transfer my photos to my computer so I could put something on Facebook; I wanted all my friends to meet my three Guardian Angels.

When I downloaded the photos, there were over 10 pictures of an area that (at the time) I thought had nothing to do with the heart attack. It was an area over by the balcony, about 50 feet east of where I collapsed (the 2nd, smaller arrow in the picture) I decided I needed to go back to the YMCA to investigate further. This time, I went straight up the stairs and it all became quite clear.

The "dream" I had been experiencing for the past month...was **NOT** a dream; it was **REALITY.** The day I died on the floor of the YMCA; I had an out-of-body experience. I'll be honest with you. **IF** anyone ever told me a story like this, I would probably think two things; either they were crazy, OR they were trying to get attention. I don't know what else to tell you...but it **DID** happen. This is what happened after I collapsed:

> *The pause button had just been pushed...on my life. I was clearly not **IN** the present. Life was at a standstill and it was eerily quiet. I was frozen in place and was viewing the scene from outside my body. A group of people were kneeling over me and I was attached to an AED. Far across the room, I could see "me" standing at the balcony, next to what appeared to be an Angel, or possibly God Himself, "hovering" next to the balcony. He was dressed in a white robe and had white hair and a beard. I could not hear the conversation, but could tell it was serious. Then...I woke up.*

I did not take this lightly, and I remind myself daily of this. Whether I have a good day or a bad day, **I COULD BE DEAD**, so I needed to make a lot of changes in my life.

I set out some goals for myself pretty early on; some were easily attainable, some were impossible, and others are...a work in progress.

REFLECTION: Wow! I came *this* close from not putting this in my book. This is the stuff that people call you "cray-cray" over. *IF* I didn't feel so sure of myself, I wouldn't have included it, however, *I AM THAT SURE IT HAPPENED*, so it made the book.

I was given a second chance in life. I believe this was an Angel sent by God to discuss my situation. *Was I ready to die?* Absolutely not! I think for some unknown reason, the Angel listened to my plea and allowed me to keep on living. The fact that I was not even a strong Christian, and this happened to me, should give a lot of people *HOPE*; that "They *DO* have a chance." If it happened to me, it can happen to anyone. I'm excited for other people to have the opportunity to grow in Christ.

Chapter 22

Cardiac Rehabilitation

Day 1, October 15, 2019: Brett (my boss...yes, the Superintendent of Schools), took me to my first cardiac rehab appointment.

I was really nervous about going to cardiac rehab. Luckily, it was in a building I was familiar with; I had been there about a year earlier trying to get some relief from low back pain (from deadlifting). I knew Molly and Jason (two Physical Therapists) because they both worked on me many times. I had never been "on the other side of the wall," because that was the cardiac rehab side.

Crystal Truex, RN BSN, was in charge of my cardiac rehab. She seemed nice enough. We had our first consultation and she explained the program. The doctor prescribed 36 sessions, so we set up all the dates and times on a calendar. I chose 7:30 a.m., the first available appointment, because I figured I could get in and out, and back to work fairly quickly. The goal was to be at work by 9:00, which never happened...it was closer to 10:00 each day, after going home and showering.

Crystal laid out the goals very clearly for the next 12 weeks. I was to attend M-W-F for an hour per day. There were three different machines that (eventually) I was to work up to 15 minutes on each; the treadmill, a recumbent bicycle, and a bike with ski-type handles that I called "the devil." The pressing motion of this machine made my sternum cut feel like it was going to break apart.

After our initial consultation, I stepped onto the treadmill. I was attempting to go 10 minutes. I was nervous but really excited to get started on ANYTHING but sitting at home. She started the machine and I began walking slowly (around 1.5 mph). Sadly, I was winded after about six minutes. She increased the speed and incline a very little bit. I could feel my lungs starting to "struggle" to get **deep** breaths. As ridiculous as it sounds, I could not focus on ANYTHING but getting a full breath. Even though the treadmill was only a little over 2 mph and less than 6 degrees of incline, it felt like ***"THIS...WAS... THE... END."***

My anxiety and fear level were a ***10***. I could not catch my breath. Crystal asked me, "How are you feeling?" I replied, ***"I feel like I'm going to have another*** *heart attack and die."* That was the end of the session; she had to pull the plug

> REFLECTION: With the exception of having my groin shaved in front of a crowd in the ER, this was the second most embarrassing thing that happened throughout this ordeal. I felt like an idiot...a failure...and a wussy. A few weeks prior, I was STRONG and although I had some blockage, felt overall pretty good. After this, I felt like part of the scene on the back of a 70's comic book, where Charles Atlas had someone kick sand in his face...or when Popeye was getting beat up by Bluto...BEFORE he ate his spinach. This was very mentally draining and created stress for me. Remember, not much gray area with me, so this was a FAILURE in my mind. Crystal told me, "You are fine and this is normal." I didn't know her...yet...so I wasn't sure what to think. I needed to look at this from a different perspective and needed to figure out how to get ahead of the curve.

I had two days to get prepared to go head-to-head with the treadmill again. I had two areas I needed to attack:

Physical/Mental: I researched blood oxygen levels and realized a pulse oximeter was going to be my "go to" tool. I purchased a $20 unit at Walgreen's. I needed to show my brain that "even when it felt like I was going to die, the pulse oximeter would not lie; it was a machine that would show EXACTLY what % oxygen I had in my blood at any given time. The goal was to have between 95-100%."

Spiritual: I reached out to Jeff Stevenson. This was hard for me to do. I had to show my weaknesses to Jeff...whom I had mentored and always preached "work ethics" and to "stay positive" all his life, and to "be a leader, NOT a follower." He sent me some motivational "go get 'em" ammo...and also a few scriptures that he recommended I put on my phone and read them aloud during my rehab sessions. I also reached out to my cousin's daughter. More on that in a bit.

I now had a plan. The next rehab session I was armed with my pulse oximeter and my scriptures. I think Crystal thought I was a bit overboard at first, but she didn't realize who she was dealing with, LOL. To say I was determined would be an understatement. She didn't necessarily think having a pulse oximeter was necessary, but...she didn't know me yet either. She quickly figured Out it was a great idea for my particular case. I OWNED the treadmill from that point on. I went about 6 minutes that day and felt great. I got in the zone and read the same scriptures over and over...and looked at my 97-98% blood oxygen levels, and did great. Physical goals came back much harder than expected. I imagined being back to lifting much sooner than it happened. I simply could not handle the pain.

REFLECTION: Again, as silly as it sounds to say I "owned" the treadmill for a whopping six minutes...it really was a MILESTONE! The pulse-oximeter played to my "no gray area" side, and the scriptures gave me confidence. I had other people that believed in me and it was making a difference. This confidence was what I needed and was a game changer. EVERYONE needs someone to believe in them and to boost their confidence, especially when they are at rock bottom. Crystal is in the perfect job. She has passion and CLEAR PURPOSE to help others and to top it off is a people person. She genuinely cares about each and every client. She would also make a great coach/trainer! I'm not sure you have picked up on the fact that ...I "may" not be the best patient to work with. LOL. She really did a great job encouraging me and building up my confidence. It was a game changer for sure.

Randy and Rhonda visited me in the hospital.

God☺: Rhonda is my cousin from Missouri. She has a daughter named Nicole. When I last visited Rhonda's house, it was about 4 years ago. Her daughters and I always hit it off, as they were complete stud athletes and we always talked about sports and workouts, etc...Nicole and I hit it off really well and I had been messaging her over the past couple of years. She was very supportive when mom passed away. She and her husband are very spiritual and I knew I needed all the help I could get, so I reached out again. She made an immediate impact with her motivational messages and scriptures. She wished (and so did I) that she wasn't 6 hours away, but she was still able to help me through tough times.

God ☺ One of the guys at cardiac rehab was very spiritual and offered many verses for me to read on my own. He was a nurse that worked for the KMC and was one of the most positive people I have ever met. His hard work motivated me and it was good to have some friendly competition.

Nicole (Randy & Rhonda's Daughter) & Jerrod with their adorable
family!
Photo Credit: Elyse Photography

Chapter 23

Nicole...Wisdom & Motivation from My Cousin's Daughter

Nicole Spencer comes from a family of "servant leaders" and she was very helpful to me...from 6 hours away throughout my ordeal. I'm so grateful for the help she gave me. To survive this type of situation, it takes all sorts of people, from all angles, to help you stay sharp and focused to overcome the many obstacles thrown at you. The biggest obstacle I had to overcome ended up being "doubt and anxiety."

REFLECTION: This is one of the most important parts of my recovery. This is NOT something you can take on alone. You need friends and family, and you need God. It's definitely a team effort. Between my Jeff's (Stevenson & Wyrick), I thought I "had this under control." Nicole introduced a new, big-time POSITIVE vibe into the equation. Don't get me wrong, I'm not sure there are two stronger men (both spiritually and physically than Jeff Stevenson and Jeff Wyrick) but this was a different and much needed perspective.

> REFLECTION: Another point I need to make: I **NEVER** believed in panic attacks or anxiety. I viewed people as "weak" when I would hear about others having these issues. Yes, this was narrow-minded thinking, but I'm sure I'm not alone in these thoughts, so I might as well share my opinion. I considered myself overall pretty "tough" both physically and mentally, but the anxiety I experienced was very real. It was not something I could just "mentally block out;" it was way more substantial than that. It truly is something that is hard to explain to someone that has NOT experienced it.

After my initial "epic fail" at the treadmill in Cardiac Rehab, I came home pretty depressed and something just told me to message Nicole. I was really reaching out more to vent and complain than anything; after all, she was 6 hours away, it wasn't like she could help me anyway. Right? That was not the case. She was as much a part of my "survival" story as anyone. I'm very grateful for all of her encouragement. She has the "heart and drive" of my mother! I'm not sure I can give a much better compliment than that. The following excerpts are from FB messages (conversations) we had over a period of time. They are personal, but *I think it is VERY important to share that even the strongest people, need to reach out for help at times.*

God☺: I explained my failure in my first day of Cardiac Rehab on the treadmill to Nicole.

From Nicole: "Yes, panic attacks are from the devil!!! It's amazing how he can get in our mind and make it race and fret. It's hard when we are already down to see how any of this can be used for good- but you are alive- ***a miracle.*** So obviously, God has something more for you. Maybe you will walk someone else through the recovery process down the road, and are experiencing all of these unpleasant things so you will know exactly how to minister to someone else. In the book of James, it says to count all of our trials as joy. Easy to read, and easy to say we can, find joy in all things, but when it comes to walking it out, it sucks and is hard to do. Jerrod and I are praying for you."

> REFLECTION: This was another turning point in my "feeling sorry for myself" routine. She was so positive and SURE of herself in believing in ME. Remember this when wondering if you should intervene in someone's life. This took 5 minutes out of her day, yet meant the world to me and ***CREATED CHANGE*** in my life.

God😊: *Nicole* messaged me. The following conversations occurred over a matter of weeks.

October 7, 2019:

She told me she had prayed for me and then asked if I had ever used the Bible app, of which I had not.

NICOLE: "No lie-the first plan it suggested for me to view today was on **anxiety** and I thought it might be a good one for you to read since you apparently have a lot of time on your hands. Jerrod and I have done several plans on this app- Francis Chan has an awesome one on the book of James and right now we are doing the Matt Chandler series on Psalm 23."

ME: "Wow. Thanks. I'm pretty beat down and once I get rested, I'll check it out. Seems a little too coincidental to not look into it. Lol. I wish I was closer to you all. It seems we would all at least be able to sit around and laugh with one another. Thanks for thinking of me."

NICOLE: " That's why I passed it on. I don't believe in coincidences!!!! Also, this morning, I was checking FB and saw a friend of my mom's post. She had some chest pain last week and got it checked out in the ER. Ended up with a stent. She had a panic attack in the early morning hours and I thought of you. She said every little twinge of anything makes her mind race and it's hard to talk yourself down after a scare like that. You aren't the only one – that should be reassuring!!!! Still sucks but you aren't a weirdo, ha-ha!!! Rest up and get stronger!

October 10, 2019:

ME: "I'm released to work Monday…1/2 days at my own pace. My blood oxygen was 98%!!! My doctor put me on a stronger med for anxiety; I don't like the last part, but also have to relax at some point."

NICOLE: "Well, that last part can be a temporary thing until you get back on your feet. Yay for half days! That will be great to get your mind back in work mode- maybe you won't be so bored."

NICOLE: "Well, the light at the end of the tunnel is in sight. Rest up, work hard and you will be back to workouts at the gym before you know it."

ME: "I hope so. I think I have a real chance at a new life with new opportunities.

NICOLE: So proud of you! Positive mindset helps in the process of recovery. You can do it!"

ME: "I need to stay positive…that's why I love talking to Rhonda and you girls. There simply are no NEGATIVES.!!!"

October 14, 2019:

NICOLE: "How did you do today?"

ME: "No problem. A bit tired, but no big deal."

NICOLE: "Sweet! Look at you go. Bet it felt good to get out and do something normal!!

ME: "Yes. Lots to catch up on but so good to be out of the house."

October 15, 2019:

NICOLE: "Well, how did work plus rehab go today?!!!!"

ME: "Work went well. Rehab was all baseline data today. EKG, BP every couple of minutes. Very disappointed on the treadmill. Six minutes in and she raised the elevation again and my breathing was sporadic. I was close to having a freak out/panic attack...when she had me show her on the chart where my breathing was, she stopped. No do overs, have to wait until Friday now."

NICOLE: "I'm sorry to hear that. You will do better Friday! And give yourself some credit-you almost died a couple of weeks ago and today you did the first exercise since then. I think six minutes is great!"

ME: "I know, just really frustrated. All vitals were perfect, just mentally weak. I've NEVER been defeated by something so simple. The devil is trying to derail me for sure. God didn't let him defeat me on Sept. 19...so I need to have more faith."

October 17, 2019:

ME: "I kept my heart rate around 127. Read scriptures the entire time and did great. It was at the Y, So not official. Tomorrow at 1:00 is rehab again...official."

NICOLE: "BOOM, BABY!!! Look at you, getting stronger. Mentally and physically! *That is AWESOME! You've just made my day.!*"

ME: "I was pretty excited...and excited to share."

NICOLE: "Absolutely- that's something to be proud of."

ME: "The pulse oximeter helped. It showed high levels of oxygen and was proof that everything was fine, breathing hurt like heck but I "scriptured it out."

ME: "This is what Jeff Stevenson sent me this morning to motivate me. It worked."

"Pray for God to give you peace in your mind and allow you to conquer your fears. Remember, he whispers because he is near! You hear the doubts because it's the devil and he has to yell to get your attention because he can't be near you." "I can do all things through Christ who strengthens me." Philippians 4:13.

NICOLE: "That's great. Now you know the pain isn't something that's going to kill you, so when it hits tomorrow (and it probably will), you won't need to panic. I will go ahead and get us signed up for a half marathon somewhere between your place and mine. I think you will be ready to hit the pavement soon."

ME: My second part of Jeff Stevenson's motivation:

"HE built you and everything else on this earth and beyond...you have to know HE is also big enough to get you through this! Go Get Em! Also tell the devil you rebuke him...AND YOU'VE CHOSEN GOD AS YOUR LORD AND SAVIOR. IT WILL SHUT HIM UP."

NICOLE: "Yes, and AMEN!!!"

October 18, 2019:

ME: "I owned the tests today. Knocked it out of the park!!! Thanks for encouragement!"

NICOLE: "YOU ROCK!" Awesome! God is good!!"

October 21, 2019:

NICOLE: "How are you doing, Dave?"

ME: "Hanging in there. I had to take something to sleep last night, so I fell asleep at 9. Long day at work full time...and an hour of cardiac rehab."

NICOLE: "Sweet! Sleep is so important and a sleep aid can hopefully be temporary. So proud of you – you are rocking it!"

I normally think of ANY drug as a "crutch" and a sign of weakness. After I experienced open-heart surgery, my view changed; if used correctly, they can be life savers. I'm not sure I would have completed my cardiac rehab without anxiety meds. Granted, it wasn't for a long period of time, however, it was at a very critical juncture.

It depends on the person...and how they manage the meds. IF it is temporary, all is well. IF it turns into a crutch, you've created another self-stressor.

REFLECTION: Nicole was such a positive influence in my recovery. Looking back through our conversations was a learning process; *BEING POSITIVE* is a learned behavior. This is who Nicole is; it didn't take a lot of time or effort from her... but look at the *DIFFERENCE* it made in my life. I'm forever grateful.

I asked Nicole for help with adding "more reading" areas to my book from Bible verses. She hadn't seen the book yet, so I gave her a list of areas I needed verses for. One area I was struggling to find verses for was "blaming God." I clearly did this throughout my life, so I wanted to cover it. She had a different approach that really hit the nail on the head. She chose some verses about how Satan is the "deceiver and adversary."

MORE READING: The following Bible verses deal with "Satan." (English Standard Version):

Peter 5:8	Corinthians 4:4
John 16:33	Job 13:15
Proverbs 3:5-6	Proverbs 28:26
Romans 8:28	

Chapter 24

The Biggest God😉 EVER! Real Life Hero

Meet Dr. Daniel Baker, a true hero!
November 11, 2019

I was finally able to meet Daniel Baker, the ER Trauma Doctor that was working out 20' from where I collapsed. He helped save my life. Coincidence? I think not. Amidst all the other **God☺'s** that occurred the morning of ***September 19, 2019***, ***THIS WAS THE BIGGEST!***

In November, I received a text from Daniel Baker, the ER Trauma Doctor that was working out at the YMCA when I collapsed...and saved my life. My primary care doctor gave him my number (his wife is best friends with her). We set up a meeting at the YMCA at 6:00 a.m. on Nov. 11th. To say I was EXCITED would be an understatement. I knew this was going to be an emotional meeting. How do you thank a man that saved your life?

November 11, 2019: I arrived at the YMCA early and waited at a table. I did not have a photo of Daniel, so I didn't know what he looked like. I was nervously sitting at the table in the lobby...wondering ... ***"Is that him?"*** each time a man walked into the facility.

Finally, he walked down the stairs (he had been working out upstairs) and said, "David?" I jumped up, shook his hand...and gave him a giant bear hug. I mean...A GIANT BEAR HUG! He was grinning ear-to-ear. I could tell he was very appreciative, **yet *SO incredibly* humble,** it was hard to believe.

We sat for 30 minutes and talked. I had him tell me from start to finish what happened on that morning. Here is the short version of things I learned a lot from our conversation.

My first question: "You must be a 5:30 a.m. workout guy also?" He said, "You know, with my schedule at the ER, I am rarely here in the mornings. I just **"happened"** to be there that day." ***God😊 God😊 God😊 God😊 God😊 God😊***

He didn't hesitate to help me, "Because it was his job." He said, "Oh, it wasn't that big of a deal; this is what I do for a living." Wow! What a humble man.

I asked Daniel to walk me through what happened that morning. He said, *'I was working out on an elliptical and happened to look your way; you fell backwards and landed on your head and back pretty hard. I knew it wasn't good. Ally (YMCA CSCS Trainer) ran to get the AED immediately. We got you hooked up quickly. You had no pulse and did not appear to be breathing. You were unresponsive for about 45 seconds and I was getting ready to shock you. I usually wait for a 5-count, even when the machine tells me to shock. I counted to 5 and you took a huge gasp for air. I waited again. About 30 seconds went by and I was getting ready to shock again. I counted to 5...and you woke up. I asked you a few questions...and then your vitals returned to normal. I knew who was on call at Wesley Medical Center (because that is where he works) so I called ahead to let them know you had some serious issues and you needed to be bumped to the front of the line. If not, with your vitals showing normal, you would have waited for hours to be treated. I told the doctor to give you a Cath test as soon as you arrived."*

We talked for a while longer and then his wife, Beth, came down the stairs with Dr. Kari. Beth teaches KG in one of our elementary schools (***God*** 😊*)* What great people. I had his wife take the photo. It was a GREAT meeting and I felt privileged to spend time with all of them that morning.

I had SO many questions for Daniel, but I knew he was a busy man so I needed to let him get on with his day. I have seen his wife several times at school, but have not had the pleasure to run across Daniel again since our meeting.

REFLECTION: Wow! What else can I say about Daniel? A very humble hero for sure. In talking with him, it was "just another day" for him and he never hesitated to get involved at all...jumped right into action.

Another "connection" we made: In my job, I have large construction projects going on ($188 million) and the person managing the projects is Jeff Hohnbaum. We talk daily about the projects, and have become good friends. Guess who he attended college with at K-State? Yep...Daniel Baker. *God*☺ What are the odds you ask? Apparently, about 1:1.

Chapter 25

The Church Experience...After Many Years

J eff Stevenson asked me to go to church with him. My normal response was, "I'm not quite ready yet." I thought back to many years ago when Dave Bycroft (local pastor in SEK) once told me "IF you are waiting to be free of sin in order to come to church, you will be waiting forever." This was in reference to me telling him, "I don't feel like I am a good enough person to attend church at this time." Remember, I was carrying a lot of hatred and was not forgiving anyone at that time, so in my mind, I wasn't ready.

I felt like I was ready at this time, so I told Jeff, "I'm not sure what to expect, but I'll give it a try." We were going to attend a place called Life Church. The pastor was broadcasting from OKC and this was a satellite site. Pastor Craig Groeschel was his name. The name sounded familiar because he was a speaker at a leadership conference held in Wichita a year ago.

Jeff came by to pick me up and I was nervous, to say the least. We were attending a 9:00 a.m. service. We arrived at the church and it was a little more laid back than what I was used to being raised Catholic. They had a band and the building held several hundred people. I grew up in a congregation of about 50 people. They had three giant video projection screens.

Pastor Tim opened the service and then three screens lit up with Pastor Craig Groeschel. I immediately liked this guy and remembered seeing him at the Global Leadership Conference, about six weeks prior to my heart attack, which was the first time I had heard of him.

We attended three Sundays in a row and I was liking it. The sermons were like they were "hand-tailored" for Jeff and me.

God☺:

Sunday #1: "Finding your Purpose." I just can't make this stuff up. It was like the pastor was speaking to ME…about my experience. This grabbed my attention fast and I was hooked.

Sunday #2: Started a series called "The Grudge." Again…he was talking to ME. This series led me to forgive my brothers, which was a big step in the right direction.

Chapter 26

Medications...Do I Dare Question My Doctors & Pharmacists?

L et's talk medications and *my opinion* of a "broken system." I'll be discussing *three* different time frames in this chapter. *First*, while in the hospital (7-10 days). *Second*, during the recovery phase (week 3-weeks 6/8), and finally what I'll call "post recovery," (months 2-4).

In the hospital, I stated earlier, that I had no idea (other than the pain meds) what they were giving me at any given time. I don't know any work around for this. Unless your wife or significant other is a pharmacist, you are out of luck. My "funny" plug here is that the woman I married for a short period of my life, was actually a pharmacist. What are the odds you say? Apparently about 1:1 with me. Anyway...back to the meds. You are at the mercy of the hospital and doctors that are treating you. When you eventually become more aware and awake, it is okay to ASK QUESTIONS. The last few days I was in the hospital, I did just that. Every time they brought me meds, I asked, "What am I taking, and what is it for?"

Recovery phase (week 3-6/8): This is where it becomes very important to *"do your research."* Please remember...it is ***very unlikely*** that your primary care doctor, who is the second doctor you will see after you get out of the hospital (the first is the surgeon) will have ***ANY direct*** communication with the surgeon. The primary care doctor will have records sent to them from the hospital. Do they read through all of them? My primary care doctor is awesome, but your mileage may vary.

The surgeon set up an appointment very early on and honestly it was very non-eventful. It's more like they wanted to admire their work and see how the scars were healing. You will ***ALWAYS*** spend more time with their assistants or nurses than with the surgeon. My consultation at 1 month (to get released to work and lift) lasted a whopping 5 minutes. It happened so fast that I forgot to ask all the questions I needed answered.

- Could I get my full release for work?
- Could I return to bench pressing?
- Did I have a limitation or restriction on weights used?
- When will the excruciating pain subside from the sternum cut?

The surgeon left the room and I left the office down a corridor...but returned to talk to the nurse. She answered all my questions.

Could I return to work? YES, no restrictions.

Could I return to bench pressing and were there any limitations/restrictions on weights?

Yes, I could return to bench pressing. Strangely enough there were "no limitations on weights," lift what you can as pain permits." Remember that last part, as it became pretty important!!! I remember trying to do pushups at first. I could only do what I call "sissy" pushups, with my knees down. Keep in mind, I was benching well over 300 pounds prior to my surgery. A year before, I was benching 350...now I could barely push half my body weight up. Another low point for sure.

What about the sternum cut pain?

The nurse told me that all my sternum pain would be gone by week 8. I don't want to call her a liar...but she was "not exactly telling the truth." I am over 8 months out presently and the sternum cut still hurts. It hurts more when going from rainy weather to heat, than it does when a cold front is moving in. I have the best of both worlds; my knee tells me when a cold front is moving in, and my chest tells me when it is going to clear up.

After seeing the surgeon, and then the primary care doctor, it was time to see the cardiologist. ***This was the most critical time to ask questions about medications, any pains, and any abnormal things going on (shortness of breath, low or high blood pressure, etc.).***

REFLECTION: Look out for yourself, as there is nobody else that is going to take as big of an interest in YOU...than YOU!" If you do ask questions and don't get answers, it is okay to switch doctors. If you don't like the way you were treated by a mechanic, I'm sure you wouldn't continue doing business with him/her. YOU are the customer and have every right to ask questions and receive answers. It is their job to explain things in a manner that you can understand. It shouldn't be your job to attempt to interpret what they are saying, just ask very specific questions and make sure you get clear answers.

Place **ALL** medications you are currently taking, over the counter or prescribed, in a Ziplock bag, and bring to **EACH** doctor's appointment. Ask them to update any meds that you are no longer taking. Ask them for a list to see what they "think" you are taking.

- Ask what each medication is for? Ask why you are taking it?

- If you know your pharmacist, and even if you don't, ask for a consultation. Ask them to verify there are no *drug interactions* with any of the medications you are taking...including over-the-counter meds.

REFLECTION: Why ask about the interactions? Won't the computer or doctors pick this up?   I was taking generic Celebrex (Celecoxib) for arthritis for over 10 years. I even had it in my bag in the hospital...and took my daily dose. I asked the nurses in the hospital, "Is it okay to take my Celecoxib and Xyzol (allergy OTC med)?" Each time I was told, "It's fine." I also took these meds with me to each cardiologist appointment. Just so you know, *NO ANTI-INFLAMMATORIES are to be taken after open-heart surgery.* A friend at work and I were talking and he said, "I don't think you should be taking anti-inflammatories after heart surgery," so I checked with my primary care physician.

Dr. Clouse indeed told me it was not suggested to take any anti-inflammatories after the open-heart surgery. The prescription I was taking, had refills on it that I had filled, and she never caught it until the pharmacy called to "renew the prescription." I stopped taking the drug and my knee hurts all the time; however, **my heart is still beating!**

Let's talk about **pain meds.** I struggled with taking the pain meds vs. not taking the meds. I mentioned in an earlier chapter that Oxycodone ended up being the "lesser of evils" when it came to pain management. My body reacted better to it than anything else, and I had less side effects. I had to take them with food or I would have an upset stomach. I also had to take them with large amounts of laxatives to offset the constipation. I took 10-12, 10mg tablets/day for several weeks after I was out of the hospital. I was willing to gamble that I would not get "hooked" on them...and did not have any trouble coming off of them. Again...not a doctor...your mileage may vary. I do not believe there is a correlation between "healing" and "being pain free." You can be in all sorts of pain and still heal...I just chose NOT to be in all sorts of pain, if it wasn't necessary. Another "self-stressor" avoided. The biggest downside to the high dosage of pain meds was the inability to operate a motor vehicle. In the end, for me, it was still the right choice.

Let's talk about **Statins**. I've been to 3 cardiologists and each of them prescribed a Statin. Here is a list of common side effects (there are a lot more than I listed):

- Muscle aches & pains
- Insomnia
- Dizziness
- Headaches
- Digestive issues

I tried 4 different statins and all 4 kept me from sleeping and all 4 made my muscles ache 100% of the time. I understand the implications of **NOT** taking the statin after a CABG (Coronary Artery Bypass Grafting). The veins they used to bypass the clogged ones "could" clog sooner without taking a statin. I also understand the implications of not being able to sleep and always being in pain. Quality of life is important to me. Don't get me wrong, I clearly do NOT want to die. An aspirin regimen is very important and recommended by all of the cardiologists. Will I try more Statins? Probably. I think as things advance; I will try again. There is enough research to support the pros vs. the cons. My latest cardiologist suggested waiting until after my 1-year check-up.

There is scary research showing the life expectancy after a CABG surgery is 10 years or less in males over 50. There are also people I know that had the surgery 20 years ago that are alive and well. Research can usually be skewed to how they want the study to go, so it is not very reliable, in my opinion.

The title of the book is "Second Chances." I know I am on borrowed time and appreciate every day that I get. I don't mean to sound like I know more than any of the doctors, because that is not the case, however, I do know my body **MUCH** better than they do. When they tell me, "The side effects you are describing are highly unlikely to happen; only a small percentage of people experience them." I'm that small percentage. It seems that even though I told the cardiologists exactly that, they ignored that fact each time.

Let's talk about ***beta blockers***. I was prescribed 50 mg/day of Metoprolol, a beta blocker, which is an "adrenaline blocker." In theory, it's an extra layer of protection for your heart. Beta blockers ***"can"*** slow down the heart and reduce blood pressure, and this ***"may"*** reduce the risk of serious events. Notice the words ***"can"*** and ***"may."*** You don't see ***"shall"*** listed anywhere. Again, your mileage may vary.

Another one of mom's favorite sayings was, "Hindsight is 20/20." I had complications from the Metoprolol starting around the 4th week after surgery. Although I was making real strides in cardiac rehabilitation, I was lethargic 24/7. I wasn't a complete "zombie" but it was close. I had zero energy and not much stamina. When I was able to go back to work full time, it was hard to stay awake at my desk in the afternoons and it was worse when I got home from work. I was asleep in the recliner by 5:00 p.m.

REFLECTION: During cardiac rehab, my maximum heart rate was to be in the 143-146 range. In "theory" the beta blocker should have prevented my heart rate from ever going higher. A small percentage of people, like me, work right through the beta blocker. I had no problem getting to 155-158 BPM...which was NOT RECOMMENDED. My PT monitored my heart rate closely and eventually, I could tell by my exertion level what my BP and HR were...or very close anyway.

By **December 1, 2019,** I was getting my strength back, as it had been a little over two months since surgery. I was still having "issues" with lethargy and low and high blood pressure.

On **December 2, 2019**, I had a passing out episode in my living room at around 5:30 a.m. I got out of bed and walked to the kitchen counter to take my morning meds. I was facing the oven clock (it showed 5:30) and opened my bottle of baby aspirin...and blacked out. I woke up about 10' from the counter. Somehow, I ended up on the other side of the recliner, lying on the floor in front of the television. I woke up, and stood up...still facing the oven clock, which now showed 5:40. There were about 299 baby aspirin all over the kitchen floor. Of course, it happened with a new bottle of 300. To say this was "concerning" is an understatement. I immediately took my blood pressure and it was normal, as was my heart rate.

I waited until 9:00 a.m. and headed to my cardiologist. They worked me in quickly. They did all sorts of tests and everything showed normal. I even asked, "Do you think the Metoprolol has anything to do with this?" The doctor answered, "No." They sent me home with a 24-hour heart rate monitor. In the event that I had an episode, I was supposed to push a button on the unit and it would record all heart rate activity. I wore it for two weeks and had no issues...not once was I dizzy or passed out. I was still tired all the time. The monitor automatically turned off the evening of **December 17, 2019.** On the evening of **December 18, 2019**, I woke up around 1:15 a.m. and thought I was having another heart attack. I took my vitals and started writing them down and documented everything that took place. It was a couple of scribbled sheets of paper. This episode was major chest pain, right trapezius pain, puking, gut pain, etc. It lasted about an hour and the pain was so bad that I took an Oxycodone. I survived but was hurting. The next morning, I drove to the cardiologist's office ... again.

This time, they told me nothing different than last time. I researched the Metoprolol and found many cases of "prescribing too high of a dosage," which led to blood pressure drops, potentially causing black outs. I was somewhat suspicious of the drug. I contacted another pharmacist and they suggested asking the cardiologist about the dosage. I asked him, and he ended up cutting it in half. I went from 50 mg/ day to 25 mg/ day.

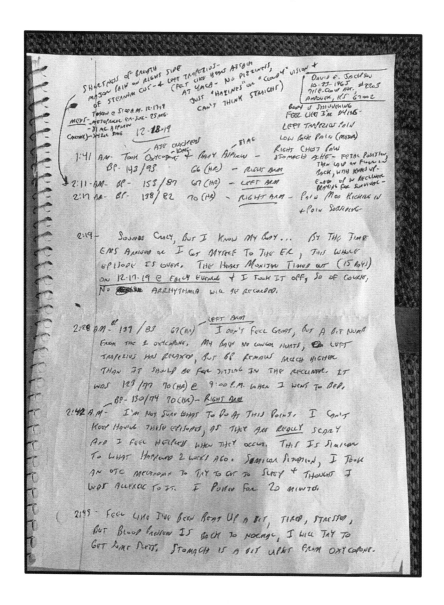

I wrote this at 1:15 a.m., on **December 18, 2019**, when I had an episode. This is me in "panic" mode. These were very scary times, and I was at a point where I felt like I needed to document EVERYTHING, since I did not feel like the cardiologists were actually believing my "stories."

A few days later, I experienced a similar situation and decided to get yet another appointment with the cardiologist. I asked for more tests, such as seeing an Electrophysiologist in case I had an "arrhythmia." Insurance would not pay for this test, unless I did a nuclear stress test first. *I scheduled that for Dec. 28, 2019 and it showed no blockage.* Insurance denied the Electrophysiologist's test. The cardiologist told me, "I'm worried for you. I do not see anything that is causing these episodes, but I believe they are happening." At least the cardiologist was honest, but I sure didn't feel very good about my future.

We discussed the Metoprolol. I told the cardiologist, "I think I'm going to stop taking the Metoprolol, since it is the ONLY thing I'm taking besides a baby aspirin, just so we can rule it out as a cause of these episodes." The cardiologist said, "I don't blame you for doing that. Let's try it." I finally asked, "What are the risks of stopping the med?" The cardiologist said, "IF you have another heart attack, the beta blocker will help lessen the damage to the heart." At this point, I figured I would take my chances. I found it interesting that cardiologists only prescribe the beta blockers for 2 years after the heart surgery.

REFLECTION: ***Since I stopped taking the Metoprolol, on December 28, 2019, I have not had ANY issues.*** My energy level came back within a few days. My workouts got stronger. This is why I say it is okay to "question your doctors." Again...I'm not a doctor...and your mileage may vary.

Chapter 27

Setting Yourself Up for Success

I n order to be successful, you have to put in the effort to achieve your goals. Over my 8 months of recovery, I learned a lot and I'm very thankful to be at this point of writing a book.

Here are some questions you need to ask yourself. Although these are in no specific order, I believe each one is of equal importance.

- *Who do you spend time with?*

  - The 3 people you hang out with the most are the culmination of "who you have become" and "how you act/behave." This isn't a revelation; it is just PURE FACT! If you claim to want to "get better" (at ANYTHING) but hang out with negative people, you are giving yourself no chance at success. Earlier in the book I referred to "self-stressors" and this is one you need to avoid and can easily do so.

- ***What is your PURPOSE?***

  - Is your purpose, just to put food on the table and to survive? Are you passionate about what you do for a living?   Do you feel like you are making a difference? Do you like your job? I think it is important to reflect on these questions and dive deeper into your own purpose.

- ***Are you self-centered or selfish?***

  - I was without a doubt the most selfish person I could think of at one point in my life. It took a heart attack to get my attention. **PLEASE** don't let it get to that point in your life. There is no room for self-serving people in any organization, company, or even a family. Don't take this wrong; ***good deeds will not get you to heaven,*** however, serving others will help keep you away from "self-stressors."

- ***When was the last time you prayed to God? When was the last time you prayed to God <u>FOR SOMEONE ELSE</u>?***

  - There is a big difference in these two scenarios. Even before my heart attack, when I would pray, it was rarely (if ever) for anyone but me (with the exception of my mother).

148

- *Have you ever felt you were not worthy?*

  - I often thought I was not worthy. This is another "self-stressor." You can look up scriptures that prove you **ARE** worthy. Jesus died on the cross next to two common criminals. He chose to hang out with them. They were worthy...***so are you.***

- *If you died today, are you spiritually ready?*

  - This is between you and God. I remember hearing a sermon from Pastor Craig Groeschel. He asked, "*Has God ever spoken to you? I often hear people talk about how God spoke to them. God told me to do this ...or God told me to do that. It seems God has spoken to a lot of people.* **God has NEVER spoken to me***...as in, I have never heard the voice of God speak to me.*" Groeschel is one of the biggest Christian leaders on the planet, with the fastest growing church in the nation...yet HE had never heard God speak to him. ***Think about that for a moment.*** This was a "relief" to me, as I thought back to EVERY prayer I'd ever prayed and NOT ONE OF THEM WAS EVER ANSWERED. This gave me a lot of confidence in Christianity and I still have a lot to learn.

- *If you are single, or even if you are with a significant other, but not married, do you have a Durable Power of Attorney?*

  - When I was admitted into the hospital back on **Sept. 19, 2019,** I had **NOTHING** in place. Please think of others in the scenario that you may be hospitalized. Don't put stress on others at that time, when it is simple to take care of this in advance.

- *If you died today, do you have a burial plan? Life insurance? Are these up to date?*

  - Again, these are not pleasant things to think about, but it creates MUCH less stress for everyone else if YOU do the work in advance. Back to the question of whether you are selfish or not? If you don't have a plan, you are being selfish. Get a plan, and make sure several people know where this information is located. It doesn't do much good to have a plan if nobody knows about it. Jeff now tells me, *"Failing to plan is planning to fail."*

If you are over 50, I recommend two things:

  - Make sure you have a primary care physician that you can trust.

150

- Ask them for a recommendation to see a Cardiologist. You can get bloodwork and a thorough check-up.

Chapter 28

The Importance of FAMILY…
During a Crisis

I alluded to the importance of family to lean on during my crisis. I could have NEVER survived this ordeal without my family.

Your *family* may look much different than mine. My family consists of close friends (all the Jeff's…Stevenson, Wyrick, Herard); Jerry & Cassandra in Bixby, OK; Steve from Bartlesville, OK; EW from Lawrence, KS; Mark B., my pharmacist friend…who was my go to guru on any medications; Mark A., Dickie; Tom & Anissa; Carol & Chad, all from Caney; Jeff R., from Indiana; Cousin Rhonda & her husband Randy from Missouri; Nicole Spencer, also Missouri…for spiritual wisdom and motivation; Brandon & Bethany, Wichita area; Grant & Fran (teachers); Austin, my former student, and Heather and Charles (teachers), all from Baxter Springs, KS; my Meadville, MO families…Shana & Karen, Jenny; even heard from Nikki today…and the list goes on. I'm sure I've left off many friends, but it is tough to remember. My Facebook family was there every day for me…and when the lights went down at the hospital, it was a relief to be able to read posts on FB.

Let's talk **work family**. In my job, this played a very large factor in my healing and recovery. I live in a 3rd floor apartment, so this presented many problems. My two administrative assistants, June and Bonnie, checked on me constantly, brought me food, and even cleaned my apartment. June even took me to the ER one time. Ted, my former Lead Maintenance, called a few times to check on me, again, all people I knew I could count on.

Donna Ray helped me understand a lot about the Bible and the power of prayer! She has a prayer group that rivals any I have seen (in truth I've never seen one, LOL), and I'm here to tell you, HER GROUP'S PRAYERS are the real deal! They made a huge difference in my recovery. They also helped me to understand the importance of praying **FOR OTHER PEOPLE!**

REFLECTION: For the first time in my life I have experienced results from **my** prayers for **other** people; I now understand how my mother must have felt her entire life. She believed in the power of prayer and put everything in God's hands. The courage she showed when she was on her death bed...now makes a lot of sense. She never showed fear...not once...and had incredible faith in God.

Ricky and his family brought me groceries and ***real*** food often. He even brought his kids over to keep my mind occupied. Everyone at Hutton was extremely supportive and they covered for me in a lot of bond meetings, as did Troy with ICON Structures. I had much support from many of my other vendor friends...really friends...that happen to be vendors...The SJCF team, SWP Tim Zoglman, 4-State Scott McLean, and Joe "all my boys play D1 football" Dinean. Lol.

Brett, my boss, hired me almost 7 years ago, when he was the Assistant Superintendent of Human Resources. When I had my heart attack, he stepped up and did so many things behind the scenes that I didn't even find out about until many weeks later. He and Brandon were the first people to show up at the hospital...after Jeff Stevenson. I'm a very picky eater, LOL, that is a given to anyone that knows me. That's really quite the understatement. I was still heavily medicated at week 3 & 4. I was not released to drive or work. Brett took my calendar with all the Cardiac Rehab appointments, and scheduled volunteers to take me to and from each one. He was first on the list. He also scheduled people to bring me groceries. I was overwhelmed with cardiac rehabilitation appointments, doctor's appointments, trying to get food, trying to get meds, etc. Since I was still taking Oxycodone, he sat in on my doctor consults and took notes, so I would know what we talked about. He is the best boss I've worked for. He is thoughtful, caring, and he put my needs over everything else at the time. I'm forever grateful.

REFLECTION: Remember when I talked about Nicole taking "five minutes out of her day" to make a difference in my life? It was very lonely in the hospital, but even more lonely when I got home. Even when I was working half days, I would get home, exhausted, and had 7-9 hours before it was time to go to bed. Anissa and Tom called a couple of times per week to "check-up" on me. These conversations were between 5-15 minutes, but took my mind completely off stressors. *Again, when you think your time doesn't matter, think again.* This mattered and was greatly appreciated!

Chapter 29

Hindsight is 20/20...Warning Signs?

1985: I had a couple of passing out episodes in my dormitory, as a Resident Assistant. I figured it was "getting up too fast" in the middle of the night. Maybe not.

1990: After a workout in an evening with Jeff Wyrick, I drove to the local convenience store to get a Gatorade. I had a "white out" spell in my truck and was disoriented for a bit. Everything was normal within five minutes.

2007-2008: This was the scariest moment. I was with Jeff Stevenson at a KU basketball game...actually, I was with Molly, Jeff's wife, because he was working the game. At halftime, I handed Molly my camera gear so I could run to the restroom. Apparently...out in the hallway, I collapsed, puked and the EMT's thought I had a heart attack. I woke up hooked to an EKG machine in the nurse's station, under the bleachers. The game was over and Jeff, Molly, and Rob Hull (another former student I coached) were looking for me. I told the EMT's who I was with and they tracked down Jeff. The EMT's wanted to transport me to the hospital and I refused services. We all went back to Jeff's apartment and I laid down on the couch for about thirty minutes and felt fine. Jeff and Rob were "not happy" with me for driving all the way back to Caney...maybe even Baxter, can't remember the exact date of this. They asked, "If the roles were reversed, would you let one of us travel after what just happened?" My answer was, "ABSOLUTELY NOT...but the roles aren't reversed." I went home. Lol. Probably not one of my finer moments.

June of 2019: I have a dear friend Brenda, in Caney, that I do work for every now and then. In 2018, I built her a privacy fence. Last summer, I was building her a deck. The lumber company showed up with my delivery around 4:30 p.m. and it was about 98 degrees. The driver was a young kid, probably 22 years old. He started unloading boards, so I helped him. We carried 2-16'x 2"x 12" boards at a time. After making two trips from the truck to the back yard, which wasn't more than 50'...I felt like I was about to die. I had to sit down and rest. It took us over 45 minutes to unload the truck...because of my lack of stamina. It was certainly embarrassing, but I really just thought, "Wow, to be young again!" I told the kid, "You are sure making this old guy feel bad. I just can't keep up with you." I sat next to Brenda on a bench...about every 5-minutes...panting like a dog. I stopped in to see Brenda a couple of months after surgery and we both thought the same thing, "What if I had collapsed and died right in her back yard?" Wow. Scary stuff for sure

Epilogue

Where do I go from here? I'm not really sure. I know I was supposed to write this book, so I can check that off my list.

The problem with deciding to write a book about something that happened 8 months ago is the difficulty in gathering information. I researched all my notes, texts messages, FB messages, etc., to try to piece all the information together the best I could. In the end, my reason for writing the book has been achieved. I think I was supposed to help people, so hopefully people will read this book, and maybe even contact me.

A couple of other things "pushed" me in the direction of writing this book. **First**, I was at my one-month appointment with my surgeon and ran into the person I replaced in my current job after he retired. He was scheduled for open heart surgery within a week. Long story, short, after about 45 minutes elapsed, I realized I just had my first "consultation" with a family. I felt like I made a difference in their understanding of the process. They had so many questions about the procedure that I had just been through, and my answers were fresh from my first-hand experience.

Second, a friend on Facebook, Bob (we haven't seen each other since jr. high...1978-ish) messaged me on ***November 9, 2019,*** and said his brother just had open heart surgery and was having an awful time with pain management and breathing. He continued messaging with questions and the answers were easy for me...very difficult to swallow for the family, but realistic. Bob told me his brother, "Felt like he was going to die and wasn't sure he could continue breathing like this." Sadly, this is normal after the procedure. I messaged Bob several times and encouraged his brother's wife to read the messages to get some peace of mind.

I said it early on in the book, "Doctors/Surgeons do a great job of "doctoring" but don't always communicate well with the patients and family members." In their defense, unless they have been through the procedure, on the receiving end, they just don't realize the pain involved. Once the drain tubes come out, there is a lot of relief, but the sternum cut is brutal no matter what.

Bob and his brother's wife, were very grateful to get some reassurance that what his brother was going through, although horrible, was considered "normal." To know I made a difference for his brother really touched my heart. I think this is an area that my book can help people with, and I hope to consult more with families in the future. The feeling of helping people is a good one. The feeling I used to get from mentoring and coaching pales in comparison to the feeling of helping a family through surviving open-heart surgery! I think this is **one** ... of my new purposes!

I mentioned that my mother was a "giver." I also mentioned that I want to be like her. When I coached and mentored kids, I had a pretty good feeling of "making a difference" and "having a purpose." As I told my story earlier, I lost that "purpose," and now it is found.

My journey took me through some really bad times; however, I had an opportunity to turn everything around and that is what I chose to do. God gave me a "Second Chance" and I am making the best of it.

Make that phone call...send that text message...post that motivational quote or scripture on FB...go out of your way to talk to that person you haven't talked to in a while...ask that person to church for the 100th time, maybe they will finally say, "yes." It only takes a minute and could change someone's day...or even their life.

This is 288 days after the heart attack at 209 pounds. Remember, I was 228 pounds a couple of weeks before my attack...and dropped as low as 190 pounds after surgery. It has been extremely difficult to put muscle mass back on my chest. It still hurts when I work out, but I'm sure it will eventually stop hurting.

162

About the Author

I'm now 54 years old, and age is just a number to me. I'm in better shape now than I've been in 20 years. I eat better, sleep better and live better...all because of my heart attack. You can be a victim or move on with your life; I've chosen to move *forward* with mine. I retire in less than two years and I plan to enjoy myself.

It's a little late to tell you this, especially after you've made it this far, but... I'm not an author. LOL. It took me precisely three weeks to write this book. I do have an English minor from 1988, but I am by no means a "writer," or reader for that matter. This book is short and to the point for a reason; if I can't read a book in an hour and a half, I usually don't pick it up. Even worse, I generally listen to audiobooks. I'm clearly also not a good salesman.

The process of writing this book was more about healing for me than anything else. The physical and emotional pain from open-heart surgery is unimaginable. I'm 9 months out of surgery and still have pain in the sternum cut each day. Workouts still hurt as do weather changes.

"Doubt" still exists, even though I no longer take my blood pressure 10 times per day and no longer carry a pulse oximeter. I do have a Coros watch that tracks my heart rate every second...and it does give me peace of mind. I set an upper limit at 152 BPM for my heart rate and the watch will about vibrate my wrist off when it exceeds the limit. Then...I rest.

As difficult as some of the material in this book was to re-hash, it was worth it. I had fun writing it and I will likely continue this as a new hobby. It was good to reflect, especially about my purpose. Thanks for reading my book and I hope it makes a difference...at least in one area of your life. If you purchase my book, please leave a review. Thanks in advance.

RECOMMENDATIONS: Two plugs for what I call *"necessary equipment."* The Omron BP710N Blood Pressure Monitor is 100% accurate and costs $40. The most accurate wrist-based HR monitoring watch I found, is the Coros "Vertix," and costs $599. I tried the Garmin Fenix 6 Pro Solar and several others, including the Apple Watch 5. In the end, "accuracy" goes to the Coros. It has a transflective screen that can easily be viewed in direct sunlight. The Coros Vertix also has a built-in pulse oximeter as accurate as any others.

Afterword

People always said I looked like my dad...I don't see it...Lol. Dad wrote many books for Phillips Petroleum; he would be proud of this one.

PLEASE LEAVE A REVIEW FOR MY BOOK ON THE SITE YOU PURCHASED FROM. THANKS IN ADVANCE.